Solving
Weed
Problems

D0109765

Solving Weed Problems

Peter Loewer

The Lyons Press

Guilford, Connecticut
An imprint of The Globe Pequot Press

The Lyons Press is an imprint of The Globe Pequot Press.

Printed in Canada
Designed by Compset, Inc.

10 9 8 7 6 5 4 3 2 1

Library of Congress Cataloging-in-Publication Data

Loewer, H. Peter.
  Solving weed problems / Peter Loewer.
    p. cm.
  Includes bibliographical references (p. 271).
  ISBN 1-58574-274-0 (pbk.)
  1. Weeds—United States—Identification. 2. Weeds—Control—United States. 3. Her-
bicides—United States. I. Title.

SB612.A2 L64 2001
632'.5'0973—dc21

                                                                    2001038091

Contents

Introduction

One man's weed may well be another man's treasure, but with few exceptions, the weeds in this book are not considered valuable to anyone. They are simply nuisances in the life of a homeowner and gardener.

Only a few of the weeds mentioned here are native plants; after all, 60 percent or more of our weeds are species introduced from other parts of the world. Some were brought in as ornamentals, which later escaped and spread from gardens into the wild. Many came in accidentally as hitchhikers with other, more valuable, seeds. Some came in the dirt ballast that kept those round-bottomed ships of the seventeenth century from rolling over in high seas when empty. And still others arrived in pants cuffs or stuck to animal hooves or the heels of boots. But, whatever their mode of transport, one way or another, they wound up in our backyards.

This book will show you how to defeat these noxious backyard invaders so that you can achieve that elusive goal: a weed-free garden.

What Is a Weed?

1

There's an old phrase that says: "Something new is always coming from Libya," and it originated long before the United States was having problems with Qaddafi. It goes back to Aristotle and his explanation for the existence of the mule. "In the dry country of Libya," he reportedly said, "there are few places where water is available, so a number of animals of various kinds will gather at the same water holes. If they are anywhere near the same size and have similar gestation periods, they just might cross, especially since there is little else to do in Libya."

The problem is not just with things coming from Libya but also with things coming in from all over. Consider the Japanese beetle, Dutch elm disease, Gypsy moths, or Mediterranean fruit flies. Then think about the hundreds of pests and diseases that are living around the world, which only plant quarantine programs prevent from entering our country. They include, among others: Andean potato latent virus, Japanese gall-forming rust, Japanese branch canker fungus, okra mosaic virus, and a multiplicity of diseases including, but not limited to, lethal yellowing disease and cadang-cadang disease.

And so it is with weeds.

"A weed is no more than a flower in disguise," wrote James Russell Lowell back in 1848. Later in that century, Ella Wheeler Wilcox (a Wisconsin pioneer poet who is also responsible for "Laugh, and the world laughs with you; Weep, and you weep alone—") picked up Lowell's thought and elaborated on it in her poem "The Weed," writing, "a weed is but an unloved flower."

"What is a weed? A plant whose virtues have not yet been discovered," wrote Ralph Waldo Emerson in "Fortune of the Republic" back in 1878.

Until recently, the tip of the hat for the best of these metaphors and similes went to Anonymous, who wrote the nursery rhyme: "A man of words and not of deeds, is like a garden full of weeds."

Then, while doing research for this book, I discovered some of the more trenchant words of John Heywood (c. 1497–c.1580) who, in addition to homilies such as "Look ere ye leap," or "Hold their noses to grindstone," also said: "Ill weed groweth fast," well before Shakespeare wrote in *Richard III*, "Great weeds do grow apace."

Obviously, Heywood had that ability to deftly "call a spade, a spade," and knew that weeds, like taxes, are always with us, and except for a few such as kudzu or wineberries, most have uncharted depths that measure at best, a few silly millimeters.

Now let me write a few good words about the United States and weeds: Most of the so-called noxious plants in this country are exotics, a word that represents plants of a foreign origin, plants that did not evolve in North America. When these plants were inadvertently (or purposely) imported into our country, all the plant baggage that originally evolved with the weed, including insect predators, diseases, specific climate restrictions, and human factors, were left back at their place of origin. So here in their new home, they literally grow in all directions with the only true limiting factor being just how much cold they can withstand.

For example, kudzu (*Pueraria lobata*) was introduced from Asia back in the early 1900s for the specific purpose of controlling erosion—it's now spreading into cities across the South, including Atlanta. Leafy spurge (*Euphorbia esula*) was introduced into the Red River Valley of North Dakota and Minnesota back in the 1880s and now this plant completely covers a vacant city lot just down the street from my house in Asheville, North Carolina. Purple loosestrife (*Lythrum salicaria*) was thought to be a great flower of Shakespeare when it began its American career back in the early 1800s, and it now covers tens of thousands of wetland acres across the country.

The problem with many weeds, especially a number of those listed below, is their initial attraction as garden

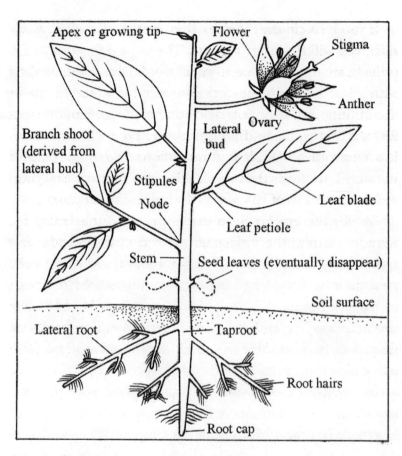

A typical plant.

plants, vines, or trees. They are botanicals that sing a siren's song about great bloom or great habit, and sometimes, as with kudzu and wineberries, great commercial potential—until it's too late to get rid of them.

If you look up the word *exotic* in *Bartlett's Familiar Quotations*, you will find nary a quote. There's a reference to Exodus (a snatch of rhyme from a Longfellow poem dealing with "The Jewish Cemetery at Newport") and a quote about "exoteric and esoteric doctrine," from Pindar, circa 250 B.C. But you'll find no notations of the word exotic as it is used to describe plant introductions from other parts of the world. Yet that's the word used to describe any new plant visitor, regardless of its value to the American continent.

So why the emphasis on exotic plants in this book? It's money: simply, the high cost of outwitting weeds that threaten agriculture, the economy, history, and our lives in general. According to K. George Beck, Associate Professor of Weed Science at Colorado State University, "in 1984, the average annual yield loss in 64 United States' and thirty-six Canadian crops caused by weeds was $7.4 billion and $909 million, respectively."

The aforementioned leafy spurge, continued Dr. Beck, reduces the number of cattle that rangeland can support in North Dakota and Montana by 75 percent and 63 percent. On millions of acres, soil and water losses mount up when grass communities replaced tap-rooted plants. Scientists found that surface water runoff and soil erosion were 56 and 192 percent higher, on land dominated by spotted knapweed, proving that this particular weed is detrimental to both soil and water resources.

When it comes to wildlife habitats, there is less documentation because research is usually conducted in areas where money is the key. But I myself was witness to a wood-land pond where cattails were slowly replaced by purple loosestrife and we watched as the population of red-winged blackbirds was decidedly reduced.

Again, in the words of Dr. Beck, "we can choose to act and invoke integrated weed management strategies to re-duce infestations and their impacts. Or, we can choose not to act and allow alien plants to continue to displace desir-able plants, thus destroying the native biological diversity of our country and the value of our grazing lands and wild lands and further negatively impact our nation's economy. It seems very unnecessary and illogical for this latter sce-nario to occur!"

So this is a book about weeds, and in most cases, what you can do to outwit them.

Please note in a bow to the number of folks who begin their lives in the Northeast and Midwest, then retire to Florida, I've included a number of plant pests that have, so far, limited their excesses to the Sunshine State, in hopes that forewarned is forearmed.

2

Chemical Herbicides

F or hundreds of years civilization has waged war on weeds. At first we all depended on hands, sticks, stones, and horse-drawn plows. As for chemicals, we stuck to sea salt to kill not only weeds but also to prevent the earth of enemies from being used for their support. Then, as a result of World War II, scientists discovered 2,4-D.

Along with the many changes in the Western world that began with the end of the war, the marketing of commercial products intensified. Today, we are barraged with advertisements of all kinds that extol the virtues of an endless line of drugs ranging from dietary supplements (usually featuring thin models) to geriatric cures (usually featuring middle-aged models) to weed killers (usually featuring healthy young suburbanites) doing battle with computerized weed monsters in the middle of gardens that are full-to-bursting with fantastic flowers and giant veggies. So I offer this first word of advice: Never buy a product based solely on its advertisement.

So what should you do? To begin with, I'm an organic gardener. The only chemicals I've ever used in my garden have been a glyphosate herbicide, an insecticidal soap, a common household spray cleaner (it's great for killing aphids), and an oil spray (again for killing insects in early spring). I have also girdled trees or rooted up the weeds by hand. If you persevere, you can probably take care of any weed problem by using one of the above methods.

But sometimes a weed that you cannot control without resorting to other chemical herbicides finds your garden. So the following are the formulations usually found in lawn and garden centers, nursery outlets, and home and hardware stores.

- 2,4-D is an effective herbicide for use on many annual and perennial broadleaf weeds, and biennials when they are in the rosette stage (for example, thistles and burdock). It's usually applied on foliage and works best when plants are young. But care must be taken because it can damage any neighboring plants if they are hit by the spray.

- CLOPYRALID is an effective herbicide for use on many broadleaf weeds, including sunflowers and thistles, members of the pea family, and the buckwheat family. It is applied as a foliar spray and translocates throughout the plant to the root system, thus reducing the potential for resprouting in perennial plants. Care must be taken because this formulation can leach into the soil and persist in the environment.

- CHLORSULFURON is an effective herbicide for use on many broadleaf weeds and also kills thistles, knapweeds, and perennial pepper weed.
- DICAMBA is an effective herbicide on many broadleaf weeds but not grasses. It is usually foliar applied.
- GLYPHOSATE is, to my knowledge, one of two reasonably safe herbicides to use in the home garden— without professional supervision. There are problems with its formulation as with any product on the market; remember, there is no perfect herbicide. For example, if it rains within six hours of applying a glyphosate herbicide such as Roundup®, its effectiveness is usually reduced. And Roundup® is not selective about what it kills. What you hit is what you destroy. When using it to control tough perennial weeds, timing of application is important. It's particularly effective on the mustard family (tansy mustard and whitetop) and sunflower family (Canada and musk thistle).

    The brother of Roundup® is Rodeo®. Formulated as a liquid, this, too, is mixed with water and a surfactant and then sprayed directly on emergent shoreline vegetation. Both are systemics that are absorbed through the leaves and then moved throughout the plant, including the roots where they break down cell activity and kill the weed. Although there are many glysophate-based products available (e.g., Roundup®), this is the only one labeled and approved for use in aquatic environments. Again, do not apply when rain is likely within six hours.

- PICLORAM is a selective herbicide that is effective on most broadleaf plants, whether annual, biennial, or perennial, but not on grasses. It will persist in the environment, however, and its use is often suggested only when other methods have completely failed. You must be doubly careful about following precautions to prevent the death of desirable plants.
- TRICLOPYR kills broadleaf weeds and some woody plants. Because it is an alkaline it can damage soft tissues, especially around the face, so care must be taken in application. It also leaches into soil.

Precautions Rule the Day

First and foremost, always consider the mechanical methods of controlling weeds before deciding on herbicides. But if you do decide to use herbicides, please follow these rules when applying chemicals to the garden:

- Protect yourself by keeping skin exposure to a minimum. Wear coveralls, not shorts, a brimmed hard hat, goggles, gloves, and boots.
- Follow package directions for cleaning your clothes and equipment before reuse. If swallowed, seek medical attention, and if none is available, call the 800 number on the package.
- Never store herbicides (or any "cides") near food.

- Read the label directions before using the product.
- Mix pesticides outside in an area sheltered from any wind. Never mix in an enclosed space.
- Never apply chemicals on a windy day. The spray can drift and hit valuable plants or drift and hit you!
- Never inhale either the dust or the spray.
- Keep children away.
- Never smoke or eat while using herbicides (or pesticides, for that matter).
- Wash your hands with soap and water after using herbicides.
- Never reuse pesticide containers.
- Dispose of containers by wrapping in newspapers and putting in the garbage for city or commercial collection.

3

Safer Ways of Fighting Weeds

Chemicals are not always the answer to getting the upper hand when fighting the battle of the weeds. A number of very effective methods of weed control have been developed over the years and here are just a few of the best. Look in the appendices for a list of suppliers.

Using Flame

Plant cells are full of sap, and sap is basically water. By the application of heat to these cells, the sap actually boils, bursts the plant's cell walls, and within seconds, the weed is history.

If you wish to enter the fiery fray, and hold up the movie *Terminator* as your role model, there is actually a BACK-PACK FLAMER KIT, which includes a 400,000 BTU torch, a three-gallon fuel cylinder, a frame to hold it all, and the delivery tubes necessary to bring the fire to the plant. All joking aside, this is a very environmentally safe method of weed control.

For a smaller garden, you can choose a smaller HAND-HELD FLAMER. This is an apparatus that uses a standard propane tank for fuel and a ten-foot hose with all the fittings that allows you to incinerate every weed you find—as long as they're in a place where there's no danger of spreading fire.

Going down the line, there is an even smaller HAND-HELD FLAMER that hooks up to any disposable propane cylinder, such as the type used on camping trips to run a small stove.

Alternative Herbicides

BURNOUT WEED AND GRASS KILLER is reported to be a non-selective herbicide that is made of all-natural ingredients, including vinegar and lemon oil. The herbicide comes as a concentrate and it's suggested that you begin spraying early in the season.

Mulch Your Way to Freedom

Many gardeners swear by mulch, not only for saving water, improving the soil, and sprucing up garden aesthetics, but also for controlling weeds. Just like your precious plants, weeds, too, need sunlight and water to grow. So today there are a number of products available that act as mulches to stifle the growing environment.

Once you decide to use mulch, I recommend that you stick to organic mulches instead of artificial or plastic materials that once spread out, must be removed by hand.

These essentially plant-based materials gradually decompose, adding organic matter to the soil. Stone mulches are also excellent, especially to keep down the weeds in those areas that separate flagstone walkways, and in rock gardens, too. The stones hold the warmth of the sun, radiating it slowly at night. And pulling up weeds from a layer of chipped or small stones is very easy.

Among the natural mulches available are shredded cedar bark, pine-bark chips, salt-marsh hay, wood shavings, wood chips, cocoa-bean hulls, licorice roots, buckwheat hulls, builder's sand, bluestone, calcined clay, baked montmorillonite clay (called Terra-green or Turface), construction gravel, and turkey grit (a crushed granite used in the poultry industry in three grades: starter, grower, and finisher). Add to this list landscaping stone, marble chips, crushed clay pots, and coal, these last often used as background color in knot gardens.

You will note that I left out peat moss in the list above. This is because peat moss is terrible mulch. After application it soon forms a waterproof mat that actually repels drops of water like sprinkled liquid on a hot griddle. In addition, peat moss is barren of any nutrients.

A word of warning: An amazing entrepreneur has decided to bring bad taste to the garden in a unique way. Today, at various landscape centers and nursery centers, mulch made of dyed wood chips is available. Instead of a neutral brown, you can now have a front yard full of orange mulch, green mulch, red mulch, and soon blue and yellow mulch.

Blanket Mulches

- BLACK POLYETHYLENE MULCHING FILM is used by many landscapers to control weeds. When planting a garden, holes can be cut in the poly to make way for transplants or seedlings, while anything else below will be starved or baked to death.
- SUNBELT WEED FABRIC is a woven material that is said to block 99.7 percent of available light, and, amazingly enough, is guaranteed to last for five years before giving in to the destructive effects of ultra-violet light.
- EWE MULCH is a biodegradable material made from wool that would normally be discarded by wool merchants. It is claimed that this mulch not only reduces weed growth, but also conserves soil moisture, and eventually breaks down, only to be turned into garden soil with increased fertility.

Hand-Held Weeding Tools

There are a number of tools for dispatching weeds, that are time-honored, made of good materials, will stand up to use, and do the job.

- THE ASIAN HAND CULTIVATOR is a hand-forged tool from Korea with an interesting, if not unique, blade design. A wood handle ends in a seven-inch steel blade that is curved and tapered to resemble a small plow. It's great for weeding.

- THE CAPE COD WEEDER is made in Maine by the Snow & Neally Company of Bangor. It's a multipurpose tool used to both weed and cultivate. It glides an inch or two under the soil surface to separate weeds from their roots and to loosen and aerate the soil. Its point can be used to pick a weed out from between two other plants or walkway stones.

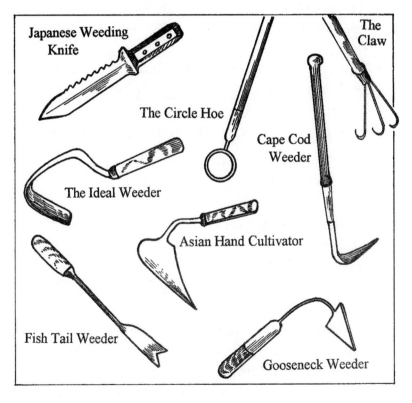

Hand-held weeding tools.

- THE CIRCLE HOE has a fifteen-inch handle that ends in a circle of steel more than two inches wide. It enables the gardener to get the weed and work the soil at the same time.

- THE CLAW consists of three hard carbon spring-steel tines and a tough ash handle that has the advantage of pulling the weeds out of the soil. A longer-handled model at twenty-four inches means you won't be forced to kneel or walk in the garden and compress the soil.

- THE FISH TAIL WEEDER AND ASPARAGUS KNIFE is made from hammer-forged tool steel, hardened and tempered to withstand rough usage. The notched blade is well sharpened and at an inch and a half, much wider than other such tools. Believe it or not, it's been manufactured in the United States since 1826 and is perfect to get the most stubborn of dandelion roots.

- THE GOOSENECK WEEDER is a short-handled version of a popular garden tool called the Gooseneck Hoe. It's the perfect design for getting between plants and between stones. The sharp triangular blade sits at the end of a curved, five-inch long neck.

- THE IDEAL WEEDER is a real old-timer, also known as a "hot bed weeder." It has a three-quarter inch blade that is well sharpened on all of its edges, including the tip. Use the tip to pick out small weeds in close spaces, or select from inches of sharp, straight, and

curved edges for your weeding and cultivating
chores.

- THE JAPANESE WEEDING KNIFE is a very useful tool for a
  variety of garden chores but is chiefly a weeder. It's a
  heavy steel blade with semi-sharp beveled edges and
  a hardwood handle. The overall length is ten inches.
- THE PICK AND PLANTER has an eighteen-inch solid ash
  handle and a heat-treated tool steel head. One end
  of that head is an unbreakable spade or trowel, and
  the other end a gardener's pick.
- THE SPEAR & JACKSON DANDELION WEEDER has a forked
  head made of high carbon steel enabling it to catch
  the taproot in its grip. You can then lever the root
  out of the ground using the handle.
- THE TRAKE is made of lightweight, solid cast alu-
  minum and combines the work of a trowel, a rake, a
  seeder, and a soil depth measure. At sixteen inches,
  the tined end is just perfect for most tap-rooted
  weeds.
- THE WEEDER/ROOTER or so-called "gold digger" out
  of the Old West has at one end a sort of mattock that
  will chip tough or weedy weeds at below ground
  level. The steel teeth on the other end will sink into
  the roots or crown of a weed, allowing you to pry it
  from the soil. The hardwood handle is fifteen inches
  long.

4

The Pollination of Weeds

Nature has a tendency to make the wonders of the vegetable world look temptingly easy to come by, especially when you forget the millions of years that often went into perfecting the slightest changes in floral structure. But add to the mix the various adaptations found in living pollinators, and you'll mutter the words of the King of Siam, "It's a puzzlement."

In order for seeds to form, the flowers must be pollinated. That can happen in a number of ways, many of which are extraordinarily clever, and all showing a high degree of sophistication.

For centuries gardeners, philosophers, and farmers have known about the relationship between pollen and the formation of fruit. Early on, Egyptian reliefs show the dusting of fruit-bearing date palm flowers with pollen. Yet hundreds of years passed before the link between the two was finally established by Rudolph Jacob Camerarius (1665–1721). In 1694, Camerarius, a German botanist and physician, demonstrated that unless pollen came into contact with a stigma, fruit would not develop. In his work, he described the stamen as the male organ and the ovary as the female organ, emphasizing their complementary relationship in the formation of seeds.

Today, after centuries of observation, we've learned a great deal about pollination and know that five pollinators carry it out, the most important being the wind (or *anemophily*). Next come the insects (*entomophily*) and the birds (*ornithophily*), followed by the relatively uncommon pollination by bats (*chiropterophily*), and finally, pollination by water (*hydrophily*).

With rare exceptions, the weeds described in this book multiply by seed.

Wind

In the spring, if you live anywhere near blooming oak trees, or gymnosperms such as pines or even yews, you know about the pollen that blows in through windows, soon coating everything with a layer of yellow dust. It's impossible to count the number of pollen grains produced by one tree, never mind many of them, so you can imagine the effectiveness of wind pollination. It may be overkill, like hitting a pin with a hammer, but from nature's viewpoint, pollen is cheap to produce.

The earliest seed plants on earth were probably pollinated by the wind, and most modern gymnosperms still are.

Today botanists think that insects pollinated the original flowering plants or angiosperms, but over the course of evolution, many of these plants turned to wind pollination.

It's easy to recognize a wind-pollinated plant. They have no nectar, flower fragrance, or brilliant colors to attract animal pollinators. Instead, their floral structure is perfectly suited to the wind. Grasses are wind-pollinated and although floral structures are still visible, they are tiny and serve no purpose. Instead, the anthers are often suspended from long filaments, hanging open to the wind and pollen. The stigmas are often feathery in appearance or branched, and all are open to the air and never protected by petals. Finally, pollen grains are usually small, very smooth, and produced in copious quantity.

Insects

Flowers that use insects as pollinators, attract them by presenting food, either nectar or pollen. Nectar is mostly sweetened water, with a 25 percent glucose level.

Usually insects are attracted to flowers by color or scent, sometimes both. Although many mammals only see in black and white, bees, for example, can see yellow, blue, and purple. And bees associate these colors with nectar.

Flowers that attract insects are usually held erect with a pronounced rim for visitors to land upon. The petals are often marked with dots or lines called nectar guides that lead to the flower's center. People and bees see different wavelengths of light, and the flower of a marsh marigold seems to be pure yellow to you or me. But to a bee, the petals have distinct lines that converge at the flower's center.

Insect-pollinated flowers are divided further into four categories: pollen flowers, bee flowers, hovering insects, and fly flowers.

- *Pollen flowers*
  Pollen flowers do not have nectar but produce a lot of pollen, and pollen is a great food for not only bees and beetles, but also other insects. Take a flashlight out to a lily flower at night, and you'll be amazed at how many insects gather there to eat. Pollen flowers include poppies (*Papaver*), roses (*Rosa*), and lilies (*Lilium*).

- *Bee flowers*
  Bee flowers (called *hymenoptera* flowers by botanists) have special adaptations so that only bees and bee-like visitors find it practical to search for nectar. On some flowers, snapdragons (*Antirrhinum*) or monks-hood (*Aconitum*) for example, the corolla is so firm that only a heavy insect like a bee or a bumblebee is heavy enough to open it. Red clover (*Trifolium)* produces the nectar so deeply within the blossoms that only bumblebees have a tongue long enough to reach the prize.

- *Lepidoptera flowers*

  Most flowers in this class are visited by insects that hover in the air while they eat. The nectar is usually hidden in spurs: the classic example is an orchid from Madagascar called the Christmas star (*Angraecum sesquipedale*). Its flower has a foot-long spur. When it was discovered, Charles Darwin predicted that an insect existed with a foot-long tongue. Some decades later, botanists found the moth, *Xanthopan*

Moth pollinating a yucca flower.

morganii praedicta, that pollinates this orchid—and its tongue *was* a foot long.

Because butterflies lack a highly developed sense of smell, butterfly flowers are often brightly colored, many with petals of pure red or pure orange. Their odor is generally light, pleasant, and very agreeable, like the smell of a meadow basking under a summer sun.

Moth flowers are usually white or at best have only faint tints, and are often drab and insignificant. Their perfume, however, is strong and heavy, often having a very sweet and soapy smell. Except for the orchids, most nocturnal flowers are tube-like, with the nectar hidden deep within the blossoms. They often close during the heat of the day.

• *Fly flowers*

With a few exceptions, fly flowers (or *dipteras*) attract insects mainly by smell—usually that of rotting carrion. Sometimes in combination with the smell they also have the color of rotting flesh. A major garden exception is the speedwell (*Veronica*), a flower that is designed to be pollinated by hover flies—and you'll be amazed to find that's exactly what shows up at these blossoms.

Favorite fly flowers are the starflowers or toadflowers (*Stapelia*) from South Africa. The fly pollinators are attracted both by hairy and dark-colored petals that often look like flesh, and a smell often described as dirty sneakers fried in rancid butter.

Birds

Bird flowers attract hummingbirds, honey-suckers, and sunbirds. Eighty percent of these flowers are red and usually very bright. They lack scent but have an abundance of nectar. About 2,000 species of birds regularly visit these flowers, and about two-thirds of these species depend on flowers for most of their food.

Bats

Bat flowers usually open at dusk. Some smell of overripe fruit while others give off the odor of mice or rats. The flowers are positioned to make it easy for bats to visit and they are often suspended on long stalks. An exception to this configuration is the saguaro cactus (*Carnegiea gigantea*). Its smell is not unattractive and the Sanborn long-nosed bat (*Leptonycteris sanborni*) approaches the flower from above, then uses its wings like parachutes, hovering over the blossom for a quick sip before flying away.

Water

Water pollination is rare but happens on occasion. One example is the popular aquarium plant, eelgrass (*Vallisne-*

ria). The plants are dioecious with male and female flowers on separate plants. As buds, the female flowers are well below the water's surface. As they mature, the flower stem (or pedicel) spirals up, eventually reaching the top and the flower floats within a dimple on the surface film. Meanwhile, tiny male flowers consisting of two stamens attached to a boatlike float are released by the hundreds and rise to the surface. They drift about until surface tension draws them into a dimple inhabited by a female flower. When the anthers touch the stigmas, pollination occurs.

5

The Longevity of Weed Seeds

The following poem first appeared in the December 1977 issue of the newsletter of the Henry Double-day Research Association, an English organization devoted to the concept of organic gardening. Lawrence D. Hills, the author, wrote it in the style of Thomas Tusser (1524–1580), an English writer known for his popular rhymed compendiums of advice for farmers.

You have in your drawer since Christmas Day,
All the seed packets you daren't throw away.
Seed Catalogues cometh as year it doth end.
But look in ye drawer before money you spend,
Throw out ye Parsnip, 'tis no good next year.
And Scorzonera if there's any there,
For these have a life that is gone with ye wynde.
Unlike all seeds of ye cabbagy kinde,
Broccoli, cauliflower, sprouts, cabbage and kale,
Live long like a farmer who knoweth good ale.

Three years for certain maybe five or four.
To sow in their seasons they stay in ye drawer.
Kohl-Rabi lasts with them and so does Pei-Tsai.
The winter "cos-lettuce" to sow in July.
But short is the life of ye Turnips and Swedes,
Sow next year only, enough for your needs.
Mustard and Cress for when salads come round.
Sows for three seasons so buy half a pound.
Radish lasts four years, both round ones and long.
Sow thinly and often, they're never too strong.
Last year's left lettuce sows three summers more.
And beetroot and spinach beet easily four.
But ordinary Spinach both prickly and round,
Hath one summer left before gaps in the ground.
Leeks sow three Aprils and one soon will pass.
And this is as long as a carrot will last.
Onion seed keeps till three years have flown by,
But sets are so easy and dodge onion-fly.
Store Marrows and Cucumbers, best when they're old.
Full seven summers' sowings a packet can hold.
Six hath ye Celery that needs a frost to taste.
So hath Celeriac before it goes to waste.
Broad Beans, French ones, Runners, sown in May,
Each hath a sowing left before you throw away.
And store Peas, tall Peas, fast ones and slow,
Parsley and Salsify have one more spring to sow.
Then fillen ye form that your seedsmen doth send.
For novelties plentie, there's money to spend.

Good seed and good horses are worth the expense,
So pay them your dollars as I paid my cents.

Obviously, when it comes to vegetables an interest in the longevity of their seeds is nothing new. (And if you are only worried about keeping popular vegetable seeds, following the instructions cited in the above poem work admirably well.) The historical record attests to this age-old interest in the life of seeds. A review of the available literature points out that the Greek philosopher Theophrastus (c.372–c.287 B.C.) mentions that "of seeds some have more vitality than others as to keeping," and "in Cappadocia [an ancient region of Asia Minor] at a place called Petra, they say that seed remains even for forty years fertile and fit for sowing."

Unfortunately, until recent years most of the research conducted on seed longevity focused on those seeds found in botanical gardens, usually stuck in dusty bins and cupboards, crammed in crumbling brown paper envelopes or those falling from dried seed pods on mounted herbarium specimens.

In 1908, in his treatise *On the Longevity of Seeds,* A. J. Ewart noted that presumably no area of human knowledge documented more misleading, incorrect, or contradictory statements than the literature dealing with seed longevity. In an attempt to establish order, Mr. Ewart divided seeds into three biological classes according to their life under favorable conditions. Microbiotic seeds have a life span not exceeding three years, mesobiotic seeds may live from three to fifteen years, and macrobiotic seeds retain viability from fifteen to over one hundred years. Under the macrobiotic classification he listed 137 species in 47 genera of the family Leguminosae (peas); fifteen species in 8 genera of Malvaceae (mallows); 14 species in 4 genera of Myrtaceae (myrtles); 3 species in 2 genera of Irideae (iris); and 1 species in each of the families Euphorbiaceae (spurges), Geraniaceae (geraniums), Goodeniaceae (goodenias), Polygonaceae (buckwheat), Sterculiaceae (sterculias), and Tiliaceae (linden or basswoods).

In her monograph *Seed Preservation and Longevity* (Leonard Hill [Books] Ltd., London, 1961), Lela V. Barton of the Boyce Thompson Institute for Plant Research, reported:

One of the earliest records of germination of old seeds is that of A. de Candolle (1846). Seeds of 368 species representing various families were collected, principally from the botanical garden of Florence in 1831, and were tested in 1846 when nearly fifteen years old. They had been kept in a cabinet protected from high humidity and extremes of temperature. Only seventeen of these species germinated when the seeds were planted in soil, and only one of these, *Dolichos unguiculatus*, showed more than fifty percent germination. Leguminosae (five out of ten species tried) and Malvaceae (nine out of forty-five species tried) accounted for fourteen of the seventeen viable lots of seeds. The seeds tested represented 180 annuals, 28 biennials, 105 perennials, and 44 woody plants, together with 11 unidentified seed lots. The author concluded that the figures obtained seemed to prove that woody species preserve their viability longer than others, and the biennials, none of which were found to be viable, deteriorated most rapidly.

In 1907, Paul Becquerel, a French botanist, tested 500 seeds found in the seed collection of the Museum of Natural History in Paris. Records showed these seeds to be between 25 and 136 years old. Four families, Leguminosae, Nymphaeaceae (water lilies), Malvaceae, and Labiatae (mints) produced germinating seeds with twenty of the seeds aged from twenty-eight to eighty-seven years old. The seeds of *Cassia multijuga* (a Brazilian tree) germinated after 158 years of storage, an apparent record at the time. Table 1 shows the results of his tests.

Mr. N. G. Moe, the head gardener of the Botanical Museum of the University of Oslo, collected seeds from 1857 to 1892 and stored the seeds in strong paper bags. He wrote the name of the species and the date on the outside. Another collection at that garden was started by A. G. Blytt, who gathered seeds during the first years of his professorship, 1880 to 1898, storing them in corked bottles. Germination tests were conducted during the years 1932 to 1933, so the ages of the seeds ranged from approxi-

Table 1

Macrobiotic spp.	Date	*% Germinated* 1906	1934	*Years of Longevity* Real	Probable
Mimosa glomerata	1853	50	50	81	221
Melilotus lutea	1851	30	0	55	—
Astragalus massiliensis	1848	0	10	86	100
Cytisus austriacus	1843	10	0	63	—
Lavatera pseudo-olbia	1842	20	0	64	—
Dioclea pauciflora	1841	10	0	93	121
Ervum lens	1841	10	0	65	—
Trifolium arvense	1838	20	0	68	—
Leucaena leucocephala	1835	20	30	99	155
Stachys nepetifolia	1829	10	0	77	—
Cassia bicapsularis	1819	30	40	115	199
Cassia multijuga	1776	—	100	158	—

mately 34 to 112 years. In all, 1,254 different groups of seeds were tested and out of these, only 53 species showed any germination. The oldest living seeds were those of a species of milk vetch (*Astragalus utriger*), at eighty-two years, giving six percent germination.

Seed from the silk tree or mimosa tree (*Albizia julibrissin*), now naturalized in the southeastern United States, was collected in China back in 1793. Deposited in the British Museum, London, the seed germinated after nearby attempts to put out a fire started by an incendiary bomb that hit the museum in 1940.

Others who have experimented with seed longevity include Mr. J. H. Turner of Kew Gardens, who, in 1933, reported viable seeds in samples of seven species of legumes that were eighty or more years of age. The genera were *Anthyllis, Cytissus, Lotus, Medicago, Melilotus,* and *Trifolium.*

Finally, back in 1948, Frits W. Went of the California Institute of Technology, and Philip A. Munz of Rancho Santa Ana Botanic Garden in California, launched an elaborate longevity test on seeds of more than 100 native California plants. Samples were dried in vacuum desiccators, then packed in small glass tubes to 0.1 millimeter of mercury or less, sealed, and placed in an insulated but unrefrigerated storage room. The last set of these samples is scheduled to be tested for germination in A.D. 2307.

Seeds Buried in the Earth

Seeds that are sealed in dry cabinets or unopened tombs in arid Egypt are one thing, but seeds that have been stored underground are another. Henry David Thoreau worked on the manuscript for "The Dispersion of Seeds" from 1860 to his death in 1862. The finished work finally appeared in the book *Faith in a Seed* (Island Press, Washington, D.C., 1933). He wrote the following about the vitality of seeds:

I am prepared to believe that some seeds, especially small ones, may retain their vitality for centuries under favorable circumstances. In the spring of 1859 the old Hunt House, so called, in this town, whose chimney bore the date 1703, was taken down. This stood on land that belonged to John Winthrop, the first governor of Massachusetts, and a part of the house was evidently much older than the above date and belonged to the Winthrop family. For many years, I have ransacked this neighborhood for plants, and I consider myself familiar with its productions. Thinking of the seeds which are said to be sometimes dug up at an unusual depth in the earth, and thus to reproduce long-extinct plants, it occurred to me last fall that some new or rare plants might have sprung up in the cellar of this house, which had been covered from the light so long. Searching there on the 22d of September, I found, among other rank weeds, a species of nettle (*Urtica urens*) which I had not found before; dill, which I had not seen growing spontaneously; the Jerusalem oak (*Chenopodium botrys*), which I had seen wild in but one place; black nightshade (*Solanum nigrum*), which is quite rare hereabouts; and common tobacco, which, though it was often cultivated here in the last century, has for fifty years been an unknown plant in this town—and a few months before this, not even I had heard that one man, in the north part of town, was cultivating a few plants for his own use. I have no doubt that some or all of these plants sprang from seeds which had long been buried under or about that house, and that that tobacco is an additional evidence that the plant was formerly cultivated here. The cellar has been filled up this year, and four of those plants, including the tobacco, are now again extinct in that locality.

Seventeen years later, what would become the longest experiment to determine the life of seeds buried in soil was begun by W. J. Beal. Mr. Beal welcomed in the year 1879 by mixing seeds of twenty different wild species with sand and burying them approximately eighteen inches below the surface. Mr. Beal used uncorked pint bottles, but their mouths were turned down to prevent their filling with water. Testing was accomplished by transferring the contents of the storage bottle to a seed flat filled with sterilized soil, then placed in a greenhouse.

After forty years of burial, seeds of eight species were still alive. These survivors were: pigweed or redroot amaranthus (*Amaranthus retroflexus*), ragweed (*Ambrosia elatior*), black mustard (*Brassica nigra*), peppergrass (*Lepidium virginicum*), the biennial evening primrose (*Oenothera biennis*), common plantain (*Plantago major*), purselain (*Portulaca oleracea*), and sour-dock (*Rumex crispus*). All produced seedlings, but after seventy years, only *Oenothera biennis* and *Rumex crispus* would germinate. Because I find the biennial evening primrose worthy of inclusion in any garden of interest, I was delighted with its pluck but, sadly, sour-dock is well named. Unless it was one of ten plants left in an otherwise barren world, it could never pass for anything but a pernicious weed.

The Seed Testing Laboratory of the United States Department of Agriculture started such testing in 1902, terminating the experiment in 1946. Seeds of 107 species, representing both cultivated and wild plants, were buried in 32 sets of flowerpots filled with sterile soil and capped with porous clay covers. They were buried at depths of 8, 22, and 42 inches. Germination tests were reported after burial for 1, 3, 6, 10, 16, 20, and 39 years. Seventy-one species germinated after one year, 61 after 3 years, 68 after 6 years, 68 after 10 years, 51 after 16 years, 51 after 20 years, 44 after 30 years, and 36 after 39 years. The highest germination rate came from the seeds buried at the 42-inch depth and the lowest from those seeds at the 8-inch depth.

After those thirty-nine years, the sixteen species with the highest germination rates were: velvetleaf (*Abutilon theophrasti*), ragweed (*Ambrosia artemisiifolia*), bindweed (*Convolvulvus arvenis*), jimson weed (*Datura stramonium*), morning glory (*Ipomoea lacunosa*), bush clover (*Lespedeza intermedia*), tobacco (*Nicotiana tabacum*), evening primrose (*Oenothera biennis*), Scotch thistle (*Onopordum acanthium*), pokeweed (*Phytolacca americana*), annual cinquefoil (*Poten-*

tilla norvegica), black locust (*Robinia pseudoacacia*), black-eyed Susan (*Rudbeckia hirta*), common nightshade (*Solanum nigrum*), red clover (*Trifolium pratense*), and common mullein (*Verbascum thapsus*).

Again, the results of this experiment will prove of no major news value to dedicated gardeners, who know about the perseverance of these plants. Because of my personal partiality to black-eyed Susans, evening primroses, and pokeweeds, I would personally choose to exclude them from being called weeds. But for centuries these plants have also been known as "the seeds of a troubled earth," usually appearing whenever dirt is disturbed after long years of lying fallow.

According to Dr. Barton, one of the most remarkable things about the longevity of weed seeds, especially when stored in the soil, is that most of them lack impermeable seed coats. Therefore, these seeds immediately absorb water when they are exposed to moist soil. That seeds, after soaking up their full measure of water, would remain viable over years of time is a remarkable fact. Apparently, these seeds do not develop a "deep" dormancy because when they are disturbed in a garden plot, they immediately begin to germinate—even if care had been taken to remove all such plants for several preceding years. Exposure to light, alternating temperatures, mechanical disturbance, or some other unknown factor just might be the stimulus that shocks these seeds to life.

Seeds from Egyptian Tombs and Other Ancients

Right up there with the mummy's curse that supposedly led to the death of Lord Carnarvon, the archeologist who uncovered Tutankhamen's tomb (more popularly known as King Tut), are stories of wheat seeds taken from mummy bindings that germinated after thousands of years. In the 1860s, Thoreau mentioned the stories of wheat raised from seed that was buried with an ancient Egyptian, and of raspberries raised from seed found in the stomach of a man in England who was supposed to have died sixteen or seventeen hundred years earlier. Thoreau generally discredited these stories because of the lack of evidence to support them.

Recent scholarship has proven that most of these seeds have undergone severe morphological and physiological degradation along with total loss of viability. While many of these seeds give evidence of their cell structure, when water is added, a great deal of disintegration occurs. Barley seeds with an age of about 3,350 years that were collected from King Tut's tomb were extensively carbonized and completely nonviable.

To date, the claim for the greatest longevity has been staked by the arctic lupine (*Lupinus arcticus*), whose seeds were found frozen and buried in the Yukon Territory of Canada. The seeds were taken from an ancient rodent burrow that contained the skull of a lemming. Carbon dating of the nests and remains of Arctic ground squirrels found buried under similar conditions in central Alaska, registered an age in excess of 10,000 years, so the researchers concluded that the seeds in the Yukon were also of this age. Even a gardener would consider such reasoning to be wildly optimistic. Knowing the perfidy of moles, I wouldn't be surprised that an enterprising Canadian member of this carnivorous genus, stopped to rest in this ancient tunnel and brushed off some seeds that were stuck to its fur.

As to other ancient seeds, between 1843 and 1855 one Robert Brown found 150-year-old viable seeds of the sacred Indian lotus (*Nelumbo nucifera*). In 1925, further tests were made but the seeds had lost the power to germinate during the intervening seventy years. Yet during the 1920s, seeds of that same species of lotus had been collected in a layer of peat in a naturally drained lakebed in Southern Manchuria and germinated. Radiocarbon tests indicated their age at $1,040 \pm 210$ years of age, making them some of the oldest viable seeds ever found. Notes taken at the time show that these seeds would not germinate without treating the hard seed coat so it would be water permeable. This was achieved by either dipping the seed in concentrated sulfuric acid or scratching it with a file.

Indian lotus seeds were also found on a submerged boat that was dated at 3,000 years of age at Kemigawa, near Tokyo. The seeds proved to be viable, but no calculations

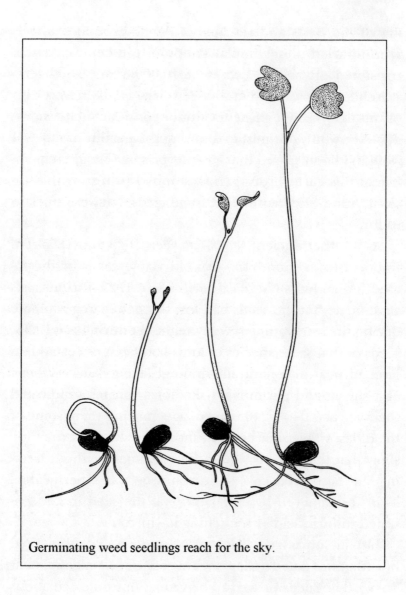

Germinating weed seedlings reach for the sky.

were made of the seeds' age and they could have settled in the mud after falling from modern plants.

Seeds of lamb's-quarters or pigweed (*Chenopodium album*) and seeds of toadflax or corn spurry (*Spergula arvenis*) were found at an archaeological dig in Denmark and were thought to be about 1,700 years of age. But there was no direct dating employed and they could have been modern weed seeds that had infiltrated the dig—or as most gardeners would believe, they were weeds and weed seeds seem to live forever.

Other seeds collected from ancient times include the species *Canna compacta*, found in an Argentinean tomb and encased in the nutshell of a species of walnut, *Jugland australis*. The walnut was part of a rattle necklace and carbon dating proved the nutshell to be about 600 years old. After germination, there was not enough of the seed for analysis, but the only way it could have gotten inside the walnut was to have been inserted there while the developing nutshell was still soft.

The Importance of the Seed Coat

The seed coat, or testa, is extremely important when it comes to seed longevity. After all, the seed coat is all that stands between the embryo and the outside world, although in some cases the fruit coat or even the endosperm can be a substitute for this structure. Usually there is an outer and inner cuticle, often impregnated with waxes or fats, then one or more layers of thick-walled, protective cells, a palisade or Malpighian layer made of heavy-walled, tightly packed, radially placed, columnar cells that are not only hard, but also horny. There are no intercellular spaces allowing water to accidentally enter the interior.

Many seeds are protected by layers of cells that contain calcium oxalate or calcium carbonate crystals, which not only protect seed embryos from the weather but from insects as well. Some seed coats contain mucilaginous cells that burst when touched with water, then provide a water-retaining barrier of protection.

When the seed detaches from the parent plant, it bears a scar called the hilum. At one end of the hilum, many species of seed bear a small hole called the micropyle but this hole remains plugged until it's time for germination to occur.

Plants from Old Seeds

Years ago, there were occasional reports about seeds that were better after a certain amount of time had passed. An *Irish Farmer's Gazette* from the mid-1800s recommended that, "The gardener knows that melon and cucumber seeds, if used of the last year's saving, produce plants too vigorous to produce much good fruit; whereas, those kept over for several years produce less rambling, but very fruitful plants." An anonymous gardener in 1932 wrote about the relative values of pumpkin seeds, claiming that in one trial, three-year-old seeds gave the best results while in another trial, four-year-olds yielded less quantity but a far higher quality fruit.

But most of the experimental evidence shows that older seed—unless properly stored—produce inferior plants.

Storing Seeds

When it comes to storing seeds, outside of using futuristic chromium tubes surrounded by helium under pressure, or any of the other super-modern methods of keeping, what should the gardener do?

First, except for a very small class of seeds known as re-calcitrant seeds, which quickly deteriorate when they lose water, most seeds are at their best when stored in a dry state. The most common recalcitrant seeds are the willows (*Salix* spp.), hazel (*Corylus avellana*), the black walnut (*Juglans nigra*), the coconut (*Cocos nucifera*), coffee (*Coffea arabica*), and wild rice (*Zizania aquatica*). But there are few guidelines here and much research waiting to be conducted. For example, wild rice is recalcitrant only when dried at temperatures below 25°F and then re-hydrated, or provided with water. But seeds will survive if dried at temperatures above 25°F and the water is provided slowly. But that seems a bit too much, so my advice, if you do have any of these seeds, is to plant them immediately and do not confine them to storage.

6

The Dispersal
of Weed Seeds

A nybody who has ever had to brush a longhaired
dog after a late autumn tramp through woods and
fields knows how some seeds travel. And if you
have been out walking that dog, you also know that seeds
become affixed to pants, skirts, and jackets, using hooks,
barbs, what looks like glue, and even natural systems of
Velcro®, in order to guarantee their being spread around
the country, if not the world. But there are many ways that
seeds spread in addition to hitching a ride on, or in, an
animal.

Wind

Small seeds often use the wind to blow them from place to
place. Some of these seeds are like dust, and like dust, they
fly through the air until eventually falling to earth. One of
the smallest seeds is a pernicious and parasitic weed called
the witch weed (*Striga asiatica*). The tiny seeds are each

only 0.0078-inch long and each plant produces hundreds of thousands of seeds. Because of their minuscule size, they can literally blow around for miles.

The seeds of most orchids are as fine as dust. Because it is so difficult for an orchid seed to find the right place to germinate and grow to maturity, each flower must produce a prodigious amount of seed to increase its chances of reproduction. A scientific count of a capsule of a *Cycnoches chlorochilon* reached the fantastic total of 3,770,000.

"The seed of cattleyas is as fine as powder," wrote Rebecca Northern in *Home Orchid Growing* (New York: Prentice Hall, 1990), "and close to a million are formed in one capsule. Its small size allows it to be carried by the gentle air currents in the jungle that are not strong enough to lift heavy particles to great heights. As the seed capsule ripens and splits open, the drift of pale yellow powder is picked up by moving air and dusted from branch to branch."

When Hurricane Hugo flew up along the southern coast, it brought a large number of various seeds of tropical plants along on the trip. Sara Peacock, a neighbor of mine whose mother lives in Charleston, South Carolina, brought me seeds from three unknown plants that sprang up in her mother's backyard shortly after the storm.

"Drifting along with the tumbling tumbleweed," goes the song, and tumbleweeds (*Amaranthus albus*) do drift and spread. When ripe and dry, these plants are torn loose from the soil, and as they blow in the wind, they drop seeds along their path.

Plumed seeds such as fireweed (*Epilobium* spp.), epiphytic bromeliads, such as the tree-dwelling *Tillisandias*, dogbane (*Apocynum*), thistle seeds (*Cirsium*), and dandelions (*Taraxacum officinale*) use their silken plumes to fly through the air, just like a badminton bird.

In every garden I've ever had there have been one of two milkweed plants, either the giant field milkweed (*Asclepias syriaca*), or the smaller, but still attractive butterflyweed (*A. tuberosa*). If you have room for such a wild plant, the giant field milkweed is worth growing because of the monarch butterfly's attraction to it, while the butterflyweed draws butterflies of all descriptions. But being milkweeds, they both produce large pods that are stuffed with hundreds of seeds, and each seed is attached to a plume of white silk. As the pod dries, it splits open, and the plumes emerge, seed-first, each waving about in the summer air. Then with a final tug at the pod, they fly off like characters in the "Waltz of the Flowers" from *Fantasia*. Children gathered plumes of the common milkweed during the Second World War, for use as stuffing in what were cheerfully called "Mae West" life preservers, which were used by the armed forces.

Some fruits that contain seeds actually have wings so they can glide through the air. Maples (*Acer* spp.), ash (*Fraxinus* spp.), elms (*Ulmus* spp.), and dock weeds (*Rumex* spp.) all have seed coats that have developed into thin wings. The airplane seed produced by an East Indian cucurbit vine (*Macrozanonia macrocarpa*) has a three-foot wing on either side of the seed, and turns in a spiral about twenty feet wide as it falls to the ground.

Many plants bear seeds that, while not being actually winged, are so flat and membranous, that they are easily carried aloft by the wind. Tulip seeds (*Tulipa* spp.), for example, have narrow marginal wings and I've watched a gentle breeze hustle them along the flat of the garden.

Lily seeds (*Lilium* spp.) are flat and packed in a seed capsule like a deck of cards. As the capsule splits, the seeds emerge a few at a time, and are blown long distances before they fall to the ground. And the same holds true for the seeds of the yucca (*Yucca* spp.).

Most of the rock cresses (*Arabis* spp.) have long, narrow pods that release elliptical seeds, each bearing a marginal wing, and fly easily in the breeze. The horseradish-tree (*Moringa pterygosperma*) is grown throughout India and bears curious three-angled, winged seeds that are discharged from a large ribbed pod about fifteen inches long, ready to float on the winds. The seeds are collected for valuable oil.

Gardeners who have watched the spread of the beautiful flowering tree called the paulownia or empress tree (*Paulownia tomentosa*) know it must be prolific. It is because in leathery, ovoid capsules are hundreds of small, delicate seeds, each of which has two or three wings, ready to cover miles in search of a place to land and germinate.

Various seeds have a seed coat that is covered with woolly hairs, and are found in willows and poplars (*Salicaceae*), cotton (*Gossypium*), kapok (*Bombax*), and anemones (*Anemone*).

The wind also disperses the seeds of many of the grasses, not because of any special adaptation but because the seeds are light and aerodynamically adapted to flying about in the wind.

Long before I read Henry David Thoreau's journals, I knew about white pines and white pine seeds. The autumn winds would toss the pine branches about with such ferocity that the cones would often fly many feet from the tree that grew them. Invariably, the cones would be empty. The oval seeds bear one long wing, and when the lid of each seed chamber lifts, the seed quickly blows away in a stiff wind or gently twirls to the ground if becalmed.

All winter long some of the cones remain high on the branches, but if you wait to collect seed from a fallen cone, the cone will be empty. Sometimes you will find the remains of a white pine cone looking like a six- to eight-inch corncob that is covered with brownish-red bristles. This is all that's left after the squirrels have completed their work. And often in late summer and early fall, you will find immature cones, still green and oozing pitch, but with every seed gone. The small birds and animals have done their job of eating. Yet there are still plenty of white pines, for nature usually—but not always—makes sure there are more than enough seeds to guarantee the survival of each species.

Water

Whether by rain, streams and creeks, sudds, or ocean currents, many seeds are distributed by water. Take rain, for instance. Very small seeds, especially if they are light in proportion to their size, will easily float. Corky seeds, such as those of the carrot family, will stay afloat for weeks at a time. The thick-walled fruits of the silverweed (*Potentilla anserina*) have been reported to float in streams for up to fifteen months. Thus, the weed is distributed along riverbanks and swampy meadows throughout the Northern Hemisphere.

The beautiful-flowered but deadly jimson weed (*Datura stramonium*) has flat corky seeds that easily float. Throughout their range, their seeds are carried downstream by floodwaters and deposited on riverbanks or along the edges of roads, where they germinate. Many sedges (*Carex* spp.) have seedpods that contain air pockets so they easily stay on top of the water, sometimes for months on end.

Marsh marigolds (*Caltha palustris*) and a number of aquatic plants or plants that live in wet places have such corky seeds. Unfortunately, the marigolds never seem to make pests of themselves but the loosestrifes, *Lythrum salicaria*, in particular, have.

In the tropics, especially in areas of heavy rain, the periodic rush of water from the mountains is awesome. It's then that millions of seeds are brought down from the heights to germinate in the plains below. Most of the time, these seed migrations are merely fortuitous, but some plants have adapted to these specific conditions. The pearl wort (*Sagina* spp.) and the mitrewort (*Mitella* spp.) have open cuplike capsules, with the seeds inside. Splashing raindrops dislodge the seeds and they wash out to the earth below.

One of the Chinese water chestnuts, *Trapa bicornis*, has blackish fruits about three inches across that closely resemble a bull's head, especially when you see the two stout, curved, sharp-pointed horns. These fruits can float great distances before sinking to the bottom of a shallow stream, where they germinate.

The Ocean

For beachcombers of all ages there is a fascinating book, the *World Guide to Tropical Drift Seeds and Fruits,* by Charles R. Gunn and John V. Dennis (New York: Quadrangle, 1976). Within its pages, hundreds of plant species are described; species that use the ocean currents to distribute their seeds, often for thousands of miles.

Known as disseminules or sea beans, tropical drift seeds and fruits all have the capacity to drift for at least one month in sea water. Viability is never a concern for the collector, because some floating seeds were never alive, some lost their vitality while drifting, while others are stranded in good condition, and immediately sprout.

Those seeds that do float are divided into five groups:

- Group 1. A cavity gives buoyancy to these seeds usually because the endosperm does not completely fill the seed. An example of this group is the sea heart (*Entada gigas*), a pantropic, high-climbing woody vine whose seeds have reached Norway from the tropics. They retain have buoyancy for at least two years, and are usually viable.
- Group 2. These seeds float because of lightweight tissue. The bay-bean (*Canavalia rosea*) has been found in most tropical currents and remains impermeable to water for at least eighteen months. The seed germinates into a strand vine, which form large tangles on tropical beaches.
- Group 3. These seeds have buoyancy because of a fibrous or corky coat, or a combination of both. An example is the country-almond or Indian-almond (*Terminalia catappa*). This native of tropical Asia has been spread by humans, by bats, and by ocean currents. The seeds float because of a very soft and buoyant seedcoat, and retain buoyancy for at least two years, with more than half of the collected seeds being viable. The seeds produce excellent shade trees and have the taste of almonds.

- Group 4. The thinness of these seeds gives them buoyancy. The best example of these is the yellow flamboyant tree (*Peltophorum inerme*), a native of the East Indies and widely planted throughout the tropics for its colorful flowers and its fine shade. The seeds will float for at least nine months, and most seeds found are viable.
- Group 5. These have buoyancy due to a combination of all the above factors. Coconuts, the fruit of the coconut palm (*Cocos nucifera*), are second largest of all known seeds and a perfect example of Group 5. While it's true that the number one spot for size goes to the so-called double coconut (*Lodoicea maldivica*), no stranded seed has ever been found to be viable. The true coconut is ranked as one of the ten most important tree species, and although Gunn and Dennis have never tested the coconut for viability, germinating stranded and drifting coconuts have been observed many times.

In the annals of drifting seeds, I cannot overlook the black mangrove (*Avicennia germinans*). The seeds belong to Group 4 but unlike most disseminules, the black mangrove usually drifts as a seedling, not as a seed. The embryo germinates while the fruit is still attached to the parent tree. When the seedling drops, it either roots in the mud below the parent tree or is carried out to sea on the tide. There is a wonderful, if not quite correct, story that the unfolded cotyledons, which are its earliest leaves, serve as miniature boats, however, floating is correctly ascribed to the buoyancy of the seedlings themselves.

Sudd

Sudd comes from the Arabic word, *sadd*, for barrier, and originally stood for the vegetation that made the White Nile an unnavigable river. Today, it refers to all those masses of dense vegetation that block water channels. A whole mass of plants, along with the seeds, can be torn away by a flood and carried downstream, usually ending up in adjacent lakes or pools. Examples of sudd plants are papyrus (*Cyperus papyrus*), water chestnut (*Trapa* spp.), water lettuce (*Pistia* spp.), and the infamous water hyacinth (*Eichornia crassipes*), which have plugged so many rivers in the Deep South.

Animals

I mentioned before the seeds that are spread about by animals, including people who go for long walks through wood and field. Their modes of transportation may be either external or internal depending on how often the seeds are used for food.

Seeds That Are Spread by Ingestion

Everyone who gardens in areas where poison ivy is found wonders why, year after year, the ivy comes back, when they know that every last vestige of this pest was removed the year before. The answer: birds eat poison ivy seeds, then expel them as they fly around the yard. There's a chink in the stone wall next to our front door and every year a chickadee inserts one sunflower seed within that crack as a hedge against tomorrow—and I'm sure others do the same around the yard.

Birds and mammals, even turtles, snakes, and tortoises, eat a number of fleshy fruits, then pass the seeds through their alimentary tracts unharmed; in fact, in many cases, the germination rate speeds up after the journey. Raspberries (*Rubus* spp.), Oregon grapes (*Mahonia* spp.), and flowering dogwoods (*Cornus florida*) are all spread about after being eaten by chipmunks, mice, birds, squirrels, and all the other inhabitants of a suburban or country backyard. Large seeds, or small seeds like grasses, can survive the digestive trip.

Many freshwater fish feed on vegetation and the seeds of water plants, then carry the seeds over long distances before they are expelled. Charles Darwin in *Origin of Species* mentioned the most curious example of this method of dispersal. Herons and other birds, he wrote, have eaten fish in whose stomachs were viable seeds of the yellow water lily. In this manner, the herons often carried the seeds many miles from their source.

The large garden snails of California and England have been know to move strawberry seeds throughout their range, and in southern climes, land crabs will eat fallen fruits and are known to spread the seed of the Malayan Otaheite chestnut (*Inocarpus edulis*).

The missel thrush has long been associated with the distribution of the European mistletoe (*Viscum album*) because the birds eat the berries. The berry's flesh contains a number of glutinous materials that are only partially digested by the bird's alimentary tract. When passed from the bird, the seeds and skins of the fruit are stuck together, and the mass frequently is securely fastened to the branches of trees. Other observers have seen mistletoe seeds stuck to the beaks of birds, who run against bark to remove them, and thus put them in position for germination.

Even the lowly earthworm has been found, upon dissection, to have a gut containing a wide variety of seeds.

Seeds Designed to Stick to Fur and Feather

Spring in our garden is not only usually evidenced by daffodils and crocuses but also, here and there, oak trees sprout because the squirrels while foraging for acorns and other nuts, moved them from one end of their territory to another, then forgot where they left them. Then, too, the ground in and around our bird feeders is always sprouting sunflowers, millet, and various grasses because of the seeds thrown about by the birds.

One spring, after gathering some seeds of hound's tongue or beggar's-lice (*Cynoglossum* spp.), Thoreau spent a long time removing them from his pocket. The following August he gave the seeds to a young lady who cultivated a flower garden. He wrote the following about the results.

[The lady's] expectations were excited and kept on the *qui vive* for a long time, for it does not blossom till the second year. The flower and peculiar odor were sufficiently admired in due time; but suddenly a great hue and cry reached my ears, on account of its seeds adhering to the clothes of those who frequented these gardens. I learned that that young lady's mother, who one day took a turn in the garden in order to pluck a nose-gay, just before setting out on a journey, found that she had carried a surprising quantity of this seed to Boston on her dress, without knowing it—for the flowers that invite you to look at and pluck them have designs on you—and the railroad company charged nothing for freight. So, this plant is in a fair way to be dispersed, and my purpose is accomplished. I shall not need to trouble myself further about it.

And the numbers of adaptations that allow seeds to stick to animals are legion. Sometimes the entire seed capsule is involved, as in the burdock (*Arctium* spp.) where the various projections are hooked at the tip. Many members of the Compositae or daisy clan, have developed barbed awns that easily stick to fur or feather. The barbed bristles of the beggarticks (*Bidens* spp.) are perfectly adapted to stick to fur, or most materials. The small flat pots of tick-trefoils (*Desmodium* spp.), are covered with hooked hairs and both get their common names from sticking like ticks, and I'm sure were the inspiration for Velcro®.

As beautiful as it is, did you ever wonder how Queen Anne's lace (*Daucus carota* var. *carota*) travels so well around the garden and fields? The seeds bear hooked bristles and easily attach themselves to any rough surface.

Many seedcoats have adapted to travel by having a gluey surface that will stick to almost anything. Seeds of the butterfly-pea (*Clitoria mariana*) are so viscid that they will adhere to any passing animal.

This group of plants include the plantains (*Plantago* spp.), weedy plants hated by people who love a perfect lawn—and with good reason because they seem to infect any green sward of grass. Like many of the rushes (*Juncus* spp.), some members of the mustard family, including the common garden cress (*Lepidium sativum*) and the shepherd's-purse (*Capsella bursa-pastoris*)—both imported from Europe—are distinguished because they become viscid when wet. Some of the flaxes (*Linum* spp.), even several genera of the phlox family, have seeds that, when wetted, emit mucilate in the form of fine threads. It's a two-way advantage. Either the seeds blow about until they reach a damp spot, where germination proceeds, or they begin their travels in damp weather, and still alight when it's best for germination to begin. And often these sticky seeds affix themselves to dried leaves and are blown about until such time that they find a place to grow.

Many grass seeds have awns or stiff hairs that actually twist and turn during periods of high humidity. The twisted portion of the awn of Porcupine grass (*Stipa spartea*), coils and uncoils as the moisture content of the air changes, causing the bent arm of the awn to revolve slowly until it comes in contact with grass stems or other objects. Then the whole seed is literally screwed down into the earth. Unfortunately, the same process occurs if the florets lodge in the wool or hair of animals, and often cause serious puncture wounds to grazing animals, usually around the eyes, nose, and mouth.

But when it comes to grabbing a tenacious hold, nothing beats the fruits of the unicorn flower or ram's horn (*Proboscidea louisianica*), an American annual from the South. The fruit lies upon the ground, with its six-inch claws sticking up into the air. When an animal steps on it, the fruit tips up and the claws clasp the fetlock. Then seeds are shed as the animal moves about.

From South Africa comes the grapple plant (*Harpagophytum* spp.), this time with woody fruits that have four wings, each cut into a number of very stout linear arms with strong hooks on the tips. Again, the hooks become attached to unfortunate animals, and as they struggle for release, the seeds fly about with ease.

Insect Carriers

I've watched a few beetles and a great many ants walking through the garden carrying seeds. One researcher has reported that fruits and seeds of more than sixty genera are carried about locally by ants, sometimes at a distance of over one hundred feet. The seeds of hellebores (*Helleborus*) are attractive to ants that will unintentionally sow them, protecting them from the rigors of winter until the following spring when they germinate.

The harvesting ants (*Messor*) of the Mediterranean region down to the Sahara, build subterranean nests that burrow ten feet or more into the ground and are topped with a dome about two feet high. The ants follow well-worn trails and go out foraging for seeds that are used to make a paste that is fed to larvae. The seeds are stored in underground granaries but if it rains and the seeds get wet, the ants take them out to dry in the sun, where some germinate.

Mechanical Dispersal

Just like the wheat that is shot from guns in order to puff up and float in milk, there are a number of seeds that depend on fruit explosions to disperse their seeds.

The plant that usually comes to mind when dealing with shooting seed is the squirting cucumber (*Ecballium elaterium*), an annual vine with fruit that is really an oblong berry about two inches long. It is native to the Mediterranean region and Linnaeus coined the genus *Ecballium,* which is from the Greek, and means "to throw" or "eject," or "cast out."

The plant has a loose trailing or prostrate habit. When the fruit is ripe, it is a bluish green, about three inches long, and hangs by a stem (or peduncle) from the vine. Suddenly, the fruit will separate from the peduncle and at the same time the fluid tension within the fruit forces the outer layers to distend and puts them under a lot of pressure. Then from the scar, the fluid contents—basically a semi-liquid mucilage—push out through the opening, carrying the

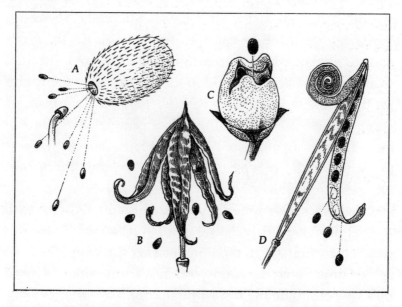

Plants that use mechanical aids for the distribution of their seeds: A. Squirting cucumber *(Ecballium elaterium);* B. Impatiens *(Impatiens aurella);* C. Witch hazel *(Hamamelis virginiana);* D. Meadow cress *(Cardamine hirsuta).*

seeds with them. This ejaculation often leads to the discomfort of the collector. While not that attractive, the squirting cucumber certainly fills the bill as a horticultural oddity.

Another plant from the gourd garden that explodes when ripe is *Cyclanthera brachystachya* (at one time it bore the species name of *explodens*). The spiny soft fruit with an up-curved end, literally breaks apart at maturity, shooting out dark brown or blackish seeds about three-eighths of an inch across.

Other garden plants use force to spread their seeds, too. One is the popular touch-me-not or snapweed, plants belonging to the genus *Impatiens*. The fleshy seed capsules are often dilated at the upper end where the seeds are borne. The walls of the capsule are elastic and as the seeds mature, pressure builds up within. Soon the five individual sections (or valves) are held together with only the slightest bit of tissue. Finally, they either part on their own, or react to the touch of another plant, animal, bird, or human. Either way, in the blink of an eye, each of the five sections rolls back like a party favor, and the seeds are thrown out to the open air.

Gardeners with greenhouses are usually familiar with the yellow-flowered creeping oxalis (*Oxalis corniculata*), a weedy inhabitant of damp floors. Using the same principle as the impatiens, the seeds are shot to the open air and quickly germinate in any favorable spot.

Many species of the geranium (*Geranium* spp.) have developed a seed distribution system based on releasing tension. Each fruit has five carpels, each containing one seed.

The carpels are all part of a long, thin column, fused together at the top. As the seeds ripen, the column begins to separate into five fibers. Finally, as tension builds, they split apart and wind up to the top like five springs. The seeds are thrown as far as ten feet.

A number of members of the legume family (Leguminosae), distribute their seeds when the fruits dry and split apart into separated spirals, sending the seeds more than eight feet. The violet-flowered Chinese wisteria (*Wisteria chinensis*) has hard, rounded seeds within a stout pod. When the pods open, seeds can fly ten feet or more.

Unfortunately for many gardeners, one of the weeds that came along in boat ballast is the spring vetch or tare (*Vicia sativa*). Here is another member of the legumes that uses exploding seedpods to send seeds traveling up to ten feet from the parent plant. But the record for flying legume seeds is probably held by the West Indian sword bean (*Canavalia gladiata*). When the large, thick pods snap open with a crack, the seeds are often thrown a distance of twenty feet.

In witch hazels (*Hamamelis* spp.) the fruit is a woody capsule with two sections or valves. When the fruit dries, it splits apart revealing two shiny black seeds within each valve. Then as the fruit continues to dry, it finally snaps apart and can discharge the seeds as far as forty-five feet, a necessary distance, or all the seeds would fall within the perimeters of the parent tree.

The small mistletoe (*Loranthaceae pusillum*) is a parasite of the black spruce and lives in the woods of the Northeast. When the berries ripen in early fall, the seeds are violently expelled. The seeds have a mucilaginous surface, allowing them to stick to other parts of the bark on either the host or a nearby tree.

The sandbox tree or monkey-pistol (*Hura crepitans*), is a tropical tree found in the West Indies, Costa Rica, and Central America. The seeds are contained in round, three-inch capsules that upon ripening, will break apart into many sections, accompanied by a sound that is heard throughout the jungle.

Humans

The final way that seeds travel around the world is in the fine hand of man. For millennia, people have traveled and carried their foodstuffs with them—including seeds of all kinds. These seeds have clung to clothing, hidden in pants' cuffs, or wound up in mud stuck to shoes.

Again, in *Origin of Species*, Darwin reported an examination and study he made of about half a pound of dried mud. He wet it and kept it covered under conditions best for germination. Within six months, no less than 537 seedlings of various species appeared. In another experiment, he took a ball of mud from the leg of a partridge, and from this raised eighty-four plants of three species.

But when it comes to reaching America, one of the easiest ways that immigrant seeds came to these shores, especially those of unwanted weed species, was in the ballast of sailing ships. Those round-bottomed boats that sailed from Europe and England left with empty holds. After all, few people in the colonies had the money to buy much of anything. Unfortunately, when empty, the ships could easily capsize, especially in storms. So for the westbound voyage, shipping companies filled the hulls with dirt, and then after landing hired men to dig it out. And guess where the dirt went? Why, along the eastern shores from Boston down to Charleston. And all that dirt was full of seeds, hence many of the alien weeds that now trouble our ecology.

7

The Worst Weed Trees in the Country

When it comes to weeds, let's begin with the biggest and work down to the smallest. The following are trees that have always been good neighbors when growing on their own turf, but when imported as exotics, for whatever reason, simply got out of hand.

Earleaf Acacia

What a romantic background the earleaf acacia, or as it's sometimes called, Darwin's black wattle (*Acacia auriculiformis*), has to its name. Native to the savannas of New Guinea, to the many islands south of Papua New Guinea, and to northern Australia, this forty-foot-tall tree is easily recognized by its sickle-shaped leaf stalks, crescent-shaped leaves, small yellow flowers, and, eventually, a crop of strange and twisted brown fruits. It was introduced to Florida as a landscape tree sometime before 1932.

With limited attention to physical needs, this acacia will flourish in a wide range of both shallow and deep soils, coral remnants, compacted clays, limestone, sand dunes, and podzols. Podzols are often severely leached, highly acidic, and generally low in agricultural value.

In Florida, where it's fast making inroads, this acacia is often found in vacant lots, waste places, roadsides, and abandoned building sites. It's also growing in undisturbed pine rockland habitats where it quickly shades out the native tree species, which then produce weak trunks and become potential wind hazards to nearby homes.

Method of Removal: Cut down adult trees and treat stumps with commercial herbicides. Do not hand-pull seedlings, but cut them off at ground level. A triclopyr herbicide can be used.

Amur Maple

The Amur maple (*Acer ginnala*) started out with great press as a small tree perfect for backyard gardens with limited space. Having but a few large branches at the base and a broad crown, almost oaklike leaves with shallow lobes, and pale yellow, fragrant flowers, this native of northern China and Manchuria was introduced into the States back in the 1860s. Reddish, two-winged fruits mature in late summer.

When young, it grows rapidly, and it requires little maintenance and does well in shade. Yet as with many plans that start with good intentions, the Amur maple has the potential to be a major weed tree. As are many other introduced species, it's stronger in many respects than native plants, and it quickly displaces native shrubs and chokes out understory trees.

Method of Removal: Cut trees at ground level and treat the stumps with a glyphosate herbicide.

Norway Maple

The Norway maple (*Acer platanoides*) is a native of Eurasia found from northern Iran to southern Scandinavia, growing on the mountains of the northern countries of Europe, and descending in some parts of Norway to the seashore. It abounds in the north of Poland and Lithuania, and is common through Germany and Switzerland. In 1683 it was introduced into Great Britain, and by 1762, the species was brought to America as an ornamental shade tree for the streets of Philadelphia.

Norway maples are fast growers and in a tolerable soil easily attain a large size (from forty to seventy feet). Because it's easily transplanted, resists drought, fights air pollution, and adapts to most pH conditions, it's the most planted street tree in the United States.

Unfortunately, though, the deep shade under its leafy canopy, and its shallow root system can be very detrimental to its environment. It damages native plants that would usually tolerate such conditions and it's almost impossible to grow grass beneath its branches. Frost cracking of its trunk is very common in areas with cold winters and it's susceptible to verticillium wilt and tar spot—two serious diseases.

Yet, it continues to be overused in the landscape.

Seeds escape from cultivation and soon invade woodlands where they out-compete native species. The smooth leaves are a shining green, as large or larger than those of the sycamore. They are seldom eaten or defaced, though, because the tree is full of a sharp, milky juice disliked by insects. In the spring, when the flowers appear, which are of a fine yellow color, this tree has great beauty.

The wood is used for the same purposes as that of the sycamore. Sugar has been made from the sap in Norway and Sweden.

Method of Removal: *Seedlings and saplings can be hand-pulled or, as they grow larger, dug up. They quickly resprout unless the roots are pulled up with the stem. Cut mature trees as close as possible to the soil surface.*

The Tree-of-Heaven

As a species, the tree-of-heaven (*Ailanthus altissima*) came to America via two routes. The first was by way of England, the trip beginning back in 1751 when Pierre d'Incarville, a French Jesuit priest, was collecting in China and mistook it for the valuable lacquer tree (*Rhus verniciflua*). He immediately sent seeds to England, one of the leading manufacturers of paints and lacquers. In 1784, the seeds were

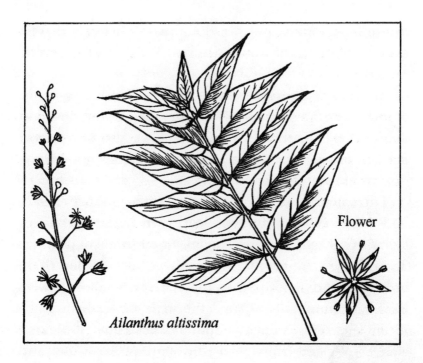

Flower

Ailanthus altissima

transported from England to America and William Hamilton, a Philadelphia gardener, introduced the species to the trade. By 1840, seedling trees were available in most nurseries. The second route involved Chinese miners. During the days of the gold rush, they brought ailanthus seeds with them as they settled in California because the tree was important to them medicinally. It was also a cultural icon.

Because of its rapid growth habits, knack for survival, and back-alley habits, ailanthus will grow just about anywhere (remember, this is the famous urban sidewalk sprouter from Betty Smith's novel, *A Tree Grows in Brooklyn*).

Away from cities, ailanthus is found growing in fields, along interstates and backcountry roads—in fact just about anywhere there's a purchase. It's also become an agricultural pest because seedlings can pop up by the dozens in recently tilled fields.

This smooth-barked tree can reach a height between 20 and 100 feet. The compound leaves are similar to those of sumac trees, and when crushed distinctly smell of peanuts. Toward the stem on the underside of each leaflet, there are two glandular-tipped teeth. The small yellow flowers bloom in June and July and the male flowers smell like dirty sneakers, hence another nickname, "stinking sumac." Winged fruits persist throughout the winter and just one tree-of-heaven can produce up to 350,000 seeds in a year. Seedlings establish a taproot three months from germination, easily outracing many native species in the competition for sunlight and space.

As if this were not enough, as do walnuts, the tree-of-heaven produces a toxin in its bark and leaves. As these poisons accumulate in the soil, they inhibit other plants. The result of these characteristics combine to make the tree-of-heaven an aggressively invasive plant, able to displace native tree and herb species. Furthermore, the root system is capable of doing damage to sewers and foundations.

Although these trees are suspected of being poisonous, possibly causing gastroenteritis in many people, and provoking a skin rash in susceptible gardeners, Asians revere it in traditional Chinese medicine. Uses include infusing the bark in water for treating diarrhea, dysentery, leucorrhoea, and tapeworm. Recent investigations have shown that ailanthus might contain at least three anti-malarial compounds.

I can personally attest to the invasive potential of this tree. Some years ago, about a tenth of a mile from my garden, a bird dropped seed picked up in another neighborhood miles away. Now I have a yearly battle ridding my property of the seedlings, which continue to sprout since I've been unable to have the mother tree removed.

And remember, tree-of-heaven is very difficult to remove once it has established a taproot. It persists in many areas despite cutting, burning, and herbicides.

Method of Removal: *Remove seedlings by hand as early as possible, preferably when the soil is moist to insure removal of the entire taproot. Larger plants should be cut; two cuttings a year may be necessary, once in the early growing season and once in the late growing season. Initially, this will not kill the plant; it will vigorously resprout from the roots, but seed production will be prevented and the plants will be lowered in stature. If continued over a period of several years, cutting during the growing season stresses the plants and may eventually kill them.*

A glyphosate herbicide, either sprayed onto the leaves or painted onto a freshly cut stump will kill the plant. To insure the herbicide gets into the root system, apply late in the growing season. Keep in mind, though, that, glyphosates are nonselective systemics and will kill all green vegetation.

The Silk Tree

The silk tree (*Albizia julibrissin*) is a fast-growing, deciduous, small tree that often reaches a height of up to thirty-five feet. The trunk is smooth and topped with an open, airy, umbrellalike canopy with graceful leaves, these being about a foot long and because of the leaflets, definitely featherlike. Each leaf has a central leaf stem with a dozen or so side branches bearing the half-inch leaflets. The leaflets fold up at night like the mimosas they resemble.

Tiny flowers are pink and arranged in compound clusters about six inches across and look like fluffy silk powder puffs. The blossoms are very fragrant by day but also produce their sweet smell for the evening garden. The flattened seeds are held in pods, four to eight inches long and an inch and a half wide.

Silk trees are naturalized from New Jersey to Louisiana and are even found in California.

Members of the Mimosaeae family, the more-than-100 species of *Albizia* are all native to Asia, Africa, or Australia. In America the trees first entered the country as seeds brought by a great plantsman André Michaux (everyone can make a mistake), who found them in Paris where they had originally arrived from China in the hands of that in-

trepid Frenchman, Pierre d'Incarville (who also introduced the tree-of-heaven into our area). Michaux started a
small nursery at Ten Mile Station north of Charleston and
by 1790 had planted those seeds that gave *Albizia* its begin-
nings in North America.

Now for the bad news: This small tree is drought tolerant, thrives in a wide range of soil conditions (including
alkaline soils), is hardy in USDA Zones 6–9, and with-
stands total neglect, as evidenced by its naturalization
throughout the southeastern United States from Washington, D.C., to Florida. They can thrive in a wide variety
of soils, produce large seed crops, resprout when dam-
aged, and have a tough taproot that quickly goes deep
into the earth.

Seedlings also come from contaminated fill dirt, so always find out where the dirt you buy comes from. These
trees produce seeds with impermeable seed coats allowing
them to remain dormant for many years. A recent study
showed that 90 percent of seeds were viable after five years
and, in a related mimosa species, a third of the seeds germinated after fifty years in open storage.

They are strong competitors to native trees and shrubs,
especially in open areas or forest edges. Dense stands of
Albizia screen sunlight and take up nutrients needed by
other plants. Silk trees tolerate partial shade but are rarely
found in forests with full canopy cover, or at higher eleva-
tions above 3,000 feet, where their intolerance of cold limits their growth.

Because the seeds are easily carried by floodwaters and swift-moving streams, seedlings can be a serious problem in riparian areas.

Method of Removal: Silk trees are controlled by a number of mechanical and chemical means. First, cut trees at ground level using a chain or manual saw. Cutting is best when flowering has started but seeds are yet to form. Because Albizias spread by suckering, resprouts are common after treatment.

Girdling the trunk is effective on large trees where the use of herbicides is impractical. With a hatchet, make a cut through the bark encircling the base of the tree, approximately six inches above the ground. Be sure the cut goes through the bark. This method will kill the top of the tree, but again, resprouting is common.

Hand-pulling will effectively control young seedlings but it must be done before that taproot starts its downward journey or you'll feel the strain of pulling in the weakest part of your back. Try this operation after a rainfall loosens the soil. Remember, the entire root must be removed since broken fragments usually resprout.

Bishopwood

Bishopwood (*Bischofia javanica*) is a native of India, Malaysia, and Polynesia that was introduced into south Florida by a nursery back in the mid-1940s where it was termed a valuable shade tree. By 1974 it was on its way to becoming a noxious weed.

Bishopswood is a large tree, reaching about forty feet in height. The dark green leaves are trifoliate with three large, leathery leaflets bearing toothed margins. Female trees produce grape-like clusters of pea-sized brown fruits.

Home includes old fields, disturbed wetlands, and tropical hardwood hammocks where it soon displaces native species. It's become a visible problem since Hurricane Andrew swept through southern Florida in 1992, removing its competition.

Since the trees are dioecious with male and female flowers on separate plants, males are not a problem. But female trees should be destroyed to keep seeds from developing and spreading.

Method of Removal: *Hand-pull young seedlings and treat older trees with a triclopyr herbicide.*

Paper Mulberry

Here's a tree that is happy to be assaulted and often killed with kindness. The paper mulberry (*Broussonetia papyrifera*) goes far back in recorded history as one of the major sources for paper as invented by the Chinese about 2,000 years ago. Before the pounding of its pulp, folks wrote upon clay tablets, parchments, and papyrus—but none of these are truly paper. According to history, the credit goes to Emperor Hi-Ti, Ts'ai Lun of Lei-Yang who first thought of the idea of pounding bark to make paper, using the mulberry tree.

As did many other trees, the paper mulberry came to America as an ornamental, immediately escaping from cultivation and is now found south to Arkansas and its neighboring states and west to Missouri.

This is a tall tree, growing to fifty feet, with a round, spreading canopy that produces an abundance of shade. The bark is gray and broad, while the oval, often lobed, leaves (rough green above and woolly beneath) are held about lightly haired twigs. Red female flowers bloom in June and are pollinated by the male flowers that appear in long structures called catkins.

Here's another one of those trees that delights in disturbed earth and, with the path of development across the country, little land near transportation routes is left undisturbed. Seedlings grow quickly but because of their tolerance of stress, soon crowd out native species.

Method of Removal: *Hand-pull small trees and cut larger trees close to the ground, then cover the remaining stumps with black plastic to prevent resprouting.*

The Australian Pine

The Australian pine (*Casuarina equisetifolia*) has a number of common names—and remember, the more common names a plant has, the more it's either revered or despised. Among the sobriquets for the Australian pine are:

she-oak, beefwood, horsetail tree, casurina, scaly bark oak, common ironwood, swamp oak, gago, goago, gagu, agoho, gaoho, agas, ngas, and the whistling pine.

Meet another problem tree from the Land-Down-Under. It's a pine tree look-alike because, from a distance, its green twigs resemble pine needles. These "twigs" are jointed and easily part to show the true leaves. Not a conifer but a member of the beefwood family, the Australian pine is a native of Malaysia, southern Asia, and the northeastern coast of Australia. Fast-growing (up to ten feet a year), seedlings soon provide dense shade above and a thick blanket of leaves below, then with maturity, layers of hard, pointed fruits. Height can eventually be 100 feet or more.

The flowers are tiny, brown, and wind-pollinated, eventually becoming a half-inch nutlet that contains winged seeds.

In the late 1800s Australian pines were brought to Florida as a shade tree, for lumber, and to plant open ditches and canals to stabilize the soil.

This tree poses many ecological threats. In Florida, Australian pines crowd out native species, including mangroves, and other plants adapted to life on the shore. Like peas, the roots of this tree are able to produce nitrogen so they easily colonize nutrient-poor soils. Eventually, the ground under this "pine" canopy becomes sterile to all introduced plants, and chemicals in the leaves can also inhibit any new plant growth around the roots. In high winds the shallow roots easily become dislodged and the trees topple over, leading to beach erosion. Finally, the plant's pollen is highly allergenic to humans.

Trees are found in the Hawaiian islands, coastal Florida, Puerto Rico, the Bahamas, and many Caribbean islands. No biological controls are currently available for management of Australian pine.

Method of Removal: Remove leaf litter and seeds. For new or small infestations, manual removal of Australian pine seedlings is recommended. Young saplings can also be hand-pulled. Larger trees can be cut down and the stumps sprayed with triclopyr herbicide. Mature trees can be killed with triclopyrs. Be sure to cut live trees since the wood gets extremely tough when dead.

Carrot Wood

Carrot wood (*Cupaniopsis anacardioides*) is a fast-growing evergreen tree of the soapberry family that reaches a usual height of thirty-five feet and is another of the many Australian imports. They were first noted in Florida back in 1955, and in 1968, the trees were introduced there as nursery offerings.

Carrot wood invades a variety of natural communities, including many of the places that make Florida unique. These include canal edges, coastal strand, cypress swamps, dunes, freshwater marshes and river banks, and sand pine scrub. Carrot wood is a special threat to coastal ecosystems such as mangrove swamps and tropical hammocks. Once introduced, it stands alone and edges out the less aggressive native plants, robbing them of light and food.

If you've ever visited the Everglades and heard locals talk about the importance of mangroves to just about everything from baby crabs to bird habitats to breeding grounds for both commercial and recreational fishing, you know just how important these trees are. Now add to the mix of hurricanes and human development, the threat of unchecked carrot wood growth and you'll know the potentially disastrous impact this tree can have.

These trees can take a salty environment, inadequate drainage, poor soil, lack of sunlight, and increased shade without halting. Some authorities think that intolerance to cold may limit distribution—but they said that about fire ants and kudzu, too.

Method of Removal: *In sandy soil the young seedlings can be pulled out by hand. Mature trees are controlled with applications of triclopyr mixed with an oil diluent.*

Eucalyptuses

I'm part of a monthly garden call-in show on Public Radio in Asheville. The first Wednesday of the month three gardeners, (Allison Arnold, Patrick Battle, and I) come to the studio to answer questions about all sorts of plants. Last February, four calls concerned a eucalyptus spotted in West Asheville.

"My heavens," we cried in unison, "where is it and we'll go out and do it in!"

The eucalyptuses (*Eucalyptus* spp.) are a major threat in warmer parts of the country. Bluegum Eucalyptus (*E. globules*) is a particular threat. It's one of Australia's most cultivated native trees, found in gardens and parks throughout that country. It's well established in the warmer parts of Europe, and does well in France, Spain, and Portugal. In California, it's so popular that many denizens believe it to be a native plant.

California was its first home upon being imported as an ornamental back in the 1870s. And it took! Yet, soon its good points far outnumbered its disadvantages. These include its heavy plant litter that acts as a suffocating mulch to emerging plants of value, its production of a waterproof carpet that prevents the soil's absorption of water, its messy bark that poses a fire hazard to nearby communities, and its falling limbs that can easily hit passersby. Obviously, these traits are major threats to many native plants and human populations.

Eucalypts belong in the Myrtaceae plant family and count among their relatives, such exotics as the *callistemons* or bottlebrushes, *leptospermum* or the tea trees, and the *syncarpias* or turpentine trees.

The bluegums are magnificent trees, often over 100 feet tall, having straight trunks, shedding bark, and very aromatic foliage. Immature stems are square and bear soft, oval-shaped leaves. Adult leaves are sickle-shaped and grow alternately on the branches. Both stages of growth are often found on the same trees. Leaves have special glands containing volatile oils that, in many species, are used commercially. Creamy white to light yellow flowers bloom from around Christmas to early May. Fruits are an inch in diameter, woody, and blue-gray. Seeds mature in around a year and usually remain on the trees until the heat of a fire or the death of the tree cause them to fall to earth.

Method of Removal: This is another stump-sprouter so even after cutting new buds appear. It's necessary to grind down the trunk to a depth of eight to ten inches, or continually monitor the stump and cut off the sprouts as they appear. For large numbers of trees use an herbicide like glyphostate.

The Figs

Everybody knows the fig of the Bible and the fig of the market, as well as the so-called strangler fig, not to mention the ubiquitous fig gracing rented condominiums and populating malls across America. They all belong to the genus *Ficus*.

The lofty fig (*Ficus altissima*) and the banyan fig (*F. benghalensis*) are invaders of southern Florida. Both have a large and spreading canopy and plenty of aerial (or prop) roots, and both, upon maturity, reach heights of fifty to ninety feet.

Imported for decoration, they came to Florida in the late 1920s. At first, these wild figs were not a problem, because the fig wasps that pollinate the fruits were not endemic to the area. So seeds never developed.

Remember that figs are something special, with the tiny flowers opening up inside the hollow center of a developing fruit. Little fig wasps hatch, then mature within the fruit (left behind by a visiting adult female fig wasp), and upon adulthood, fly from fig to fig, carrying bits of pollen, thus pollinating other flowers in their path.

There is a different species of fig wasp to pollinate every species of fig. For a long time the only fig wasps in America were those that pollinated edible figs. But at some time in the last century, somebody or something brought a new species of wasps to Florida (and Hawaii), and among them were the pollinators of the lofty and the banyan fig. (There is evidence that fig wasps can either fly great distances or be carried along by speedy atmospheric winds.) Whatever their mode of transport, they are here.

Wild animals eat the figs, and seeds wind up in the strangest places, including tree crotches, cracks in pavements, and house foundations. Seeds germinate, and if germination occurs up in a tree, the figs, being epiphytes, produce aerial roots that stretch to the ground. If not eliminated, the roots crack foundations, usually kill the host trees, and produce lots of shade, hurting less aggressive native plants.

As for the edible fig (*F. carica*), they've been in the Americas since the 1700s, and while limited to fig nurseries, were not a problem. But like everything else in the world, they've spread and now pose a threat, again crowding out native species.

Method of Removal: Figs can be killed with applications of triclopyr herbicides but care must be taken not to kill the host trees. When small, edible figs are easily uprooted by hand. As they grow, they become more difficult to control and must be cut down, but keep in mind that these trees will send up new shoots.

The Cajeput Tree

From Australia came the cajeput or paperbark trees (*Melaleuca quinquenervia*), arriving in the early 1900s. The half-inch gray-green, lance-shaped oval leaves of this tree are arranged alternately along the stem and smell of camphor when crushed. Flowers are white, brushlike spikes and the fruits are small, woody, button-like seed capsules.

Trees reach a fifty-foot height, and have a thick and spongy white bark. A mature tree can produce more than a million seeds per year and store an estimated twenty million. Seeds are dispersed by wind and water.

Native to Australia, New Guinea, and New Caledonia, the Cajeput tree was imported in order to dry up swamps, thus opening soggy Florida land for development and agriculture. Back in the early 1930s, a developer actually hired an airplane to drop seeds into the Everglades wetland system. And today we're spending billions to put it back the way it was.

Why drop the seed? Well, it seems that *Melaleucas* have an evapo-transpiration rate approximately four times that of native saw grass. Since 1960, the range of this invasive species has increased greatly. By 1980, it had infested thousands of acres—or about 6 percent of the total land area of southern Florida.

Melaleuca is a fast grower in Florida's heat and quickly established itself in the saw grass marshes, on lakesides, along creek banks, and canals. Upon maturity, the trees form dense stands of nearly impenetrable branches. According to Florida conservationists, in one year, one paperbark tree can produce an island hammock up to 600 feet in diameter.

Method of Removal: *Both seedlings and saplings can be pulled up by hand. Chainsawing larger trees or girdling the trunks are good methods for the control of this species. The herbicide imazapyr has proven to be effective, also.*

The Chinaberry Tree

Chinaberry trees (*Melia azedarach*) are major pests in much of the Southeast. Listed in Category I of invasive plants of Florida (and for good reason), chinaberries were introduced into Georgia and South Carolina back in the early 1800s—and they spread. Today they are threats to eleven states, including Texas and Hawaii.

They are deciduous trees with two-foot long, alternate leaves, divided into toothed and pointed leaflets, of a dark green color. Leaves have a characteristic musky odor. Tree height is about fifty feet or sometimes is more of a shrub.

The lilac-colored flowers are small but numerous and bloom in large terminal clusters. The yellow (and sticky) fruits persist through the winter. In Florida, the fruits ripen in late summer and early fall.

Birds love the seeds and so the trees spread with ease. These hard, shiny seeds are often used for beaded jewelry and for rosaries. Extracts from the bark and fruit have pharmacological properties and are used in China to kill parasitic roundworms. And note, all parts of the tree are poisonous (especially to turtles), leading to stomach irritation, vomiting, bloody diarrhea, paralysis, irregular breathing, and respiratory distress. But authorities say that it's toxic only with the ingestion of large amounts—but never say what constitutes a large amount.

In addition to the threat to humans (and turtles), these invasive trees are another example of exotics being tough and overpowering and a special danger to native species.

Note: From Central India comes a relative of the chinaberry, *Azadirachta indica*, commonly called the neem tree and the source of today's popular health elixir, neem oil. This oil has been used for centuries to treat skin disorders as well as fungus and plant diseases.

Method of Removal: *This tree is truly a seed machine with majestic output. The only good chinaberry is a dead chinaberry. Use the systemic herbicide triclopyr.*

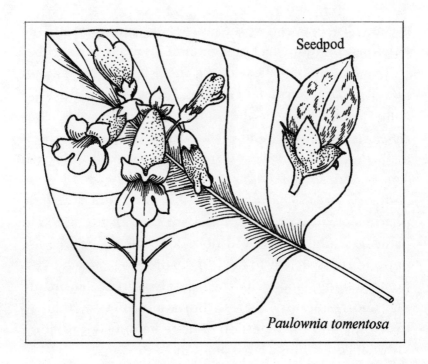

Seedpod

Paulownia tomentosa

The Empress Tree

In ancient Chinese legend, the empress tree (*Paulownia to-mentosa*) was considered to be an omen of good fortune. It was associated with the Phoenix, that mythical bird that re-generates itself in fire (probably because this fast-growing behemoth often sends up new shoots after the tree is cut or burns down). However, unlike the dawn redwood (*Metasequoia* spp.) or the gingko (*Ginko biloba*), two trees from the same homeland that have found accepted residence in America, the paulownia has not—despite its charming legend.

To add to their charm, paulownias are used in China to promote the growth of hair and to also prevent its graying. A leaf tea was also used as a foot bath for swollen and aching feet. But please note, this tree contains potentially toxic compounds. More investigations must be made before its use as a medicinal can be recommended.

Finally, its wood is highly esteemed in Asia because of its many unique qualities. It's reportedly capable of withstanding repeated soakings and subsequent drying out so it's popular for coffins, fences, and roof applications. The wood is soft and brittle when fresh, becoming hard and strong after harvest, so it's especially useful for carving. In fact, the first tea leaves arrived in North Carolina, packed in beautifully carved boxes made of paulownia.

Because of the prodigious amount of seeds, paulownias spread and have been naturalized in various parts of the world. In the early 1800s, crates of breakable cargo were shipped from China using the rounded seed pods as packing material. Once the crate was opened, the seeds blew to the four winds.

While paulownia is an invasive weed threatening native lands in much of the American Southeast, it's acceptable in warmer parts of the world since it grows in poor soil and what is usually termed wasteland.

Adventurous southern gardeners often use it as a pollarded shrub. With its stunning large leaves it makes quite a statement as a specimen plant. By cutting the tree to the ground every year, in the spring, twelve- to fifteen-foot stems arise from a central point and carry leaves often up to two feet long.

Interest is growing in the use of paulownia as a timber crop to replace the decline of tobacco. It is such a valuable and fast-growing timber tree that in years past, poachers in helicopters would cut trees from the woods of western North Carolina because each trunk was worth thousands of dollars.

Method of Removal: *Unless starting a tree plantation, remove the seedlings as they appear or you will shortly be overrun and forced to spend more and more money in tree removal as they grow larger and larger.*

White Poplars

The white poplars (*Populus alba*) grow along river banks, fields, parks, wastelands, in good soil and in poor soil—in fact almost everywhere in the country. Trees grow rapidly and reach mature heights of seventy-five to ninety feet.

When I lived on an old farm in Sullivan County, New York, there were four huge white poplars planted along the driveway. They managed to be tall and rangy, sent out a multitude of suckers, and put forth water-seeking roots that soon found the nearby septic tank. About the only good thing to say for these trees concerned early spring visits of a very large porcupine who sat high up in the tree closest to the nearby driveway and looked out upon the melting snows and mud of spring.

The bark of the white poplar is light gray with darker gray patches that spread around the trunk in bands. Leaves are somewhat triangular, shiny green on top and covered with a white fuzz underneath. The long stems allow the leaves to wave about in the winds, so the color of the tree seems to change as you watch.

Flowers appear in two- to three-inch pendulous catkins with male and female blossoms on separate trees. Catkins usually appear in late March and April. Once mature, the tufted seeds fly out on the wind, carried aloft by long silky, white hairs that look like small wads of cotton.

Brought to America from central and southern Europe, ranging east to western Siberia and central Asia, white poplars arrived in 1748 with colonial settlers. The poplars were planted as street and landscape trees, and on farms.

Today they are threats because of competition to many native plants, taking over fields and abandoned lands. In addition, these trees are subject to many diseases and thanks to those flying seeds, can sprout up anywhere. White poplars are found in forty-three states throughout the continental U.S.

Method of Removal: Seedling trees should be pulled up as soon as they are spotted. Make sure you get all the roots because even small root-bits can resprout. Cut mature trees as close to the ground as possible, treating the remaining stump with continued doses of glyphosate. Mature trees can also be girdled, killing the tree by cutting off its food and water supply. Using a hatchet or saw, make a cut through the bark encircling the base of the tree, about six inches above the ground and deep into the bark.

Black Locust

We have a few black locusts in our garden where it borders the nearby lake. When blooming in May, the fragrant, white, pealike flowers hang down in exotic bunches of bloom, and they are things of beauty. But when the suckers advance, producing legions of strong saplings, each armed with razor-sharp thorns, this thing of beauty becomes a painful threat to both life and limb.

Black locusts (*Robinia pseudoacacia*) are medium-sized, usually short-lived trees, natives of the Southeast, and deciduous. Mature height ranges from forty to sixty feet but on sites with good soil and plenty of rainfall, trees can reach heights of up to 100 feet.

The bark is thick and deeply furrowed and the branches usually bear sharp spines. The compound leaves have seven to seventeen rounded leaflets making compound leaves up to a foot long. The white flowers bloom from May into June, eventually forming reddish pods from three to four inches long. Unfortunately, the shallow roots, which grow in all directions, produce endless sprouts.

The original natural range of black locusts concentrated in the central Appalachian Mountains from central Pennsylvania and southern Ohio south to northeastern

Alabama, northern Georgia, and northwestern South Carolina, the Ozark Plateau of the Southeast.

Years ago, when the black locust was harvested, not only for firewood, but for its strong and close-grained wood that was used for railroad ties, tool handles, insulator pins, boxes, fenceposts, and wooden toys, problems with spreading were few. But at the same time that these uses were on the decline, the trees were planted to reestablish worn-out woodlands, raped landscapes, and similar areas of neglect. So today, black locusts are a serious threat to native vegetation way outside of their natural habitats. Once introduced into an area, black locusts grow and spread like there's no tomorrow, taking room and light from more timid native plants. And there's more: with the bee population on the decline, the big blossomy blooms of the black locust compete with native plants for pollinators.

Method of Removal: Wear protective clothing and cut, cut, cut. Cutting sprouts will eventually kill the parent tree. Remember to brush some glyphosate herbicide on the stumps.

Chinese Tallow Tree

Imagine, we have Ben Franklin to thank for introducing (back in 1776) the Chinese tallow tree or popcorn tree (*Sapium sebiferum*) to America. For years it had a great reputation as a decorative tree and as a fine source of bird food.

This is a small- to medium-sized deciduous tree, up to thirty-five feet tall, having a gnarled trunk with gray to whitish gray bark, and vertical cracks. Alternate leaves are oval and broad, rounded at the base, and turn orange to scarlet in the fall. Flowers are greenish yellow, blooming in terminal spikes about three inches long and ripen from September into October, developing into three-lobed fruits that resemble perfect popcorn. The flowers are favorites of honeybees and the fruits are eaten by birds. The average tree can produce about 100,000 seeds. Needless to say, these are invasive trees.

Broken stems produce a milky juice that is mildly poisonous, as is the unripened fruit, which can cause skin irritation and if eaten, probable battles with stomach complaints and diarrhea.

Today the range is Florida, up the Atlantic coast to North Carolina, and east to Texas, and even southern Arizona.

Again, these trees have no natural enemies in America and spread like wildfire. The result is just another assault on native plants.

Method of Removal: Pull seedlings by hand. If cut when mature, the trees sprout with ease so a herbicide is necessary for control. Triclopyr is recommended.

Queensland Umbrella Tree

The Queensland umbrella tree or the octopus tree (*Schefflera actinophylla*) is another native of Australia that captured the American houseplant, office building, and shopping mall markets because of its ease of cultivation and ability to grow under low light levels.

Indoors in a pot it's generally harmless (although it can be irritating to sensitive skin), but outside in southern Florida, and in Hawaii, the tree becomes an aggressive thug, with roots that penetrate, then spread, and eventually support a very large tree, up to forty feet tall.

The shiny green leaves consist of seven to sixteen leaflets, and resemble an open umbrella while the flowers, if blooming, look like radishes that split open to many stamens.

Birds are its sowers and like the figs, schefflera seeds can land in tree crotches, germinate, grow, then send roots to the ground below, allowing them to invade all sorts of outdoor territories. Again, like most exotics, they compete with native plants for light, room, and nutrients.

Method of Removal: Pull up seedlings by hand. Older trees can be cut at ground level, then the stumps treated with a triclopyr herbicide.

Tamarisk

According to The Nature Conservancy, tamarisks are members of the Tamarisk Family (Tamaricaceae) but there is some dispute regarding the correct scientific naming of the deciduous species of tamarisk now at large and invading western North America. So while open to future corrections, we are dealing with the following three species: *Tamarix ramosissma, T. chinensis,* and *T. parviflora.*

Commonly known as tamarisks, or the saltcedars, these tall shrubs or small trees are often found growing along streams and rivers out West, where they form tightly woven masses of stems, the branches and offshoots of trees often up to thirty feet tall. Recent classifications list the species as among the worst Ten Most Noxious Weeds in America.

Small, scaly leaves (like those of cedars), about one-sixteenth of an inch long, clasp the stems, giving a light and airy look to the plants. In the right environment (near salt water), they are often encrusted with salty secretions.

Tamarisks bloom with plumes of many small, four- or five-petalled flowers of white or pink. Each little flower produces thousands of tiny seeds, usually spread by wind power. They can also spread by water.

Originally, tamarisks were natives of the Mediterranean region, and east to China and Japan. In the early 1800s, they were introduced to America, both as ornamentals (some nurseries still sell them as innocents), and to plant along river and stream banks to control erosion.

By the turn of the last century, plants began to escape—and spread. Today, according to various conservation agencies, they grow unchecked on some 1,000,000 acres, primarily in Texas, Utah, New Mexico, and are on the increase in California.

It's a beautiful plant and does its job in controlling erosion, so what's the problem? You've heard it before: Tamarisks crowd out native plants (including food for wildlife), and in so doing, choke waterways, use up precious water without any returns, and are especially dangerous because the roots can tolerate brackish and salty water by releasing built-up salts through its leaves. In addition, while flash fires will kill most natives, the roots of tamarisks just sprout again.

Method of Removal: Because they are so deep rooted and maintain a great "flushing system" (based on their ability to remove salt), chemical control is tricky. With mass infestations, trees should be cut to the ground then the stumps sprayed with systemic herbicides. But that's an often difficult (and dangerous) process for the homeowner.

Because of this difficulty, there are current investigations underway testing biological controls, including a gall midge, a moth, and a leaf beetle. Until better methods are available, though, the best way is still pulling up small seedlings by hand.

Siberian Elm

The Siberian elm (*Ulmus pumila*) is just another tree that was introduced into America because of its fast growth and ease of planting. And like many such trees, it was a big mistake.

The Michigan State University Extension sums up this tree as "a fast growing, weak-wooded tree often sold to homeowners as a cheap 'instant shade' tree. The fast growth does not overcome the tree's deficiencies of weak wood and nuisance insects."

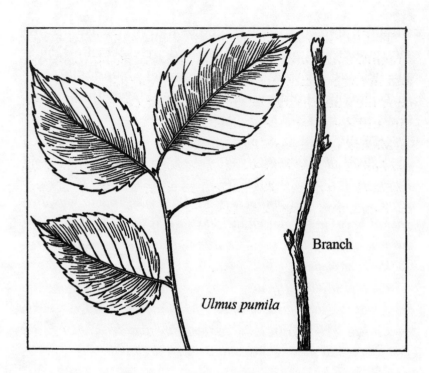

Branch

Ulmus pumila

Siberian elms have an open silhouette, large ascending branches, and pendulous branchlets. Originally from northern China and eastern Siberia, this species is resistant to the Dutch elm disease. Along with its disease resistance, another factor in its popularity is the tree's ability to stand up to the dirt and pollution of an urban existence.

Among its faults are the weakness of its wood (leading to endless fallen branches), the persistence of its seedlings, powdery mildew, leaf spot, the ravages of the elm leaf beetle, and the persistence of the seeds, which are blown about by the winds.

The trees are found both in dry and moist soils, along streams, in pastures, in abandoned fields, along roadsides, and in forlorn city lots. Like the white poplar, they are acceptable when young, but unlike many trees, lose both dignity and appearance with age.

Method of Removal: *Pull up seedlings with a vengeance. If you have time, and the trees are fairly mature, you can girdle the trunks (late spring to early summer). Finally, cut them and treat the stumps with a glyphosate herbicide.*

8

Weedy Shrubs

Invaders are not limited to trees. The following plants usually grow as bushes or shrubs (a bush being a low-growing and thick shrub without a distinct trunk).

Japanese Barberry

The Japanese barberry (*Berberis thunbergii*) is a dense deciduous shrub, growing between three and six feet tall. Small rounded leaves are usually red or green (there are many cultivars available) and grow from spiny branches. Pendant flowers are small and yellow, developing into bright red berries in late summer.

Shrubs were introduced into America in the late 1800s as a landscape plant. Today it is found wild in much of the Northeast and I've spotted it while walking backcountry trails in western North Carolina.

Because it grows equally well in sun or shade, these bushes not only invade open fields and pastures but are also soon at home along woodland margins, and eventually enter the forest proper. Once established, they shade out native plants, depriving the wildlife dependent on such plants of their natural food. Their spines are hazards, too, and collect all sorts of blowing leaves and trash (including plastic grocery store bags, which are becoming endemic throughout the woods of the Northeast and Southeast).

Method of Removal: *Pull seedlings and small or shallow-rooted plants when soil is moist. Larger plants must be dug up, and make sure you get all the roots. Larger bushes can be carefully cut down and the stumps painted with a glyphosate herbicide.*

Scotch Broom

Scotch broom (*Cytisus scoparius*) is such a lovely plant that it's difficult to believe it's considered an invasive exotic. Unlike most of our unwanted introductions, this plant arrived by way of Hawaii, islands that are usually perceived as being under attack and not part of the offensive.

Captain Walter Colquhoun Grant, who was gifted of some seeds by the British consul in Hawaii, introduced this particular broom to the West Coast. In 1850, Grant planted the seeds on his thirty-acre farm on the southern coast of Canada's Vancouver Island. Some 150 years later, the Scotch broom has a roothold in some two million acres in Oregon, Washington, and down to California.

Brooms have been introduced into Australia, Chile, India, Iran, New Zealand, and South Africa.

Brooms are airy and attractive shrubs, about five feet tall, with whiplike branches that bear tiny leaves and in the spring, thousands of bright yellow (sometimes orange or red) pealike blossoms. The fertilized flowers develop into pods that hold up to nine seeds, of a type called "seeds of the troubled earth." These are seeds that may lie dormant for several decades waiting for just the correct amount of moisture coupled with land disturbances that will instigate germination. Seedlings shoot up in newly exposed dirt and can resist drought over long periods.

Like most exotics, brooms crowd out native plants. This habit, plus their inherent attractiveness, and their ability to fix nitrogen in poor soils (using nitrogen-fixing bacteria hosted by root nodules), makes them a triple threat. They also easily resprout from stumps, and have a life span of fifteen to twenty years (or more).

Brooms also pose an additional threat because they easily ignite in forest fires carrying the flames up to the tree canopies where fire burns faster and hotter.

Method of Removal: *Dispatch seedlings whenever spotted. Cut through existing patches with a brush hog, but you must keep at it to get the new sprouts. A controlled fire will work with some infestations but obviously must be done only under controlled conditions. While triclopyr and some other herbicides have had limited success, this chemical removal is yet to be encouraged.*

Russian Olive and Autumn Olive

For years I grew Russian olive (*Elaeagnus angustifolia*) in my garden up north in Sullivan County, New York. I was aware that the tree seeded about a bit, but I kept growing it because it was so tolerant of poor soils and matured quickly into a large shrub or a small tree, which by the age of four or five years, actually looked ancient.

A native of southeastern Europe and western Asia, Russian olive came to America as an ornamental in the late 1800s, quickly escaping from gardens into the wild. A usually thorny shrub or a tree, older specimens can reach a height of thirty feet. The ability to grow in poor soil depends on the plant's ability to fix nitrogen in its roots, and with this gift, it can grow just about anywhere.

All sorts of conservation folks and gardeners meant well when they suggested planting Russian olives to control erosion, establish windbreaks, and provide food for wildlife. Today Russian olives are found from Pennsylvania to Virginia, then west and south to North Carolina.

The stems, the fruits, and the undersides of the deciduous lance-shaped leaves have coverings of silvery, sometimes rusty-red scales. Plants begin to flower, fruit, and seed at three years of age. Very fragrant, creamy yellow flowers appear in June and July and develop into abundant silvery fruits.

In the early 1900s, autumn olive (*Elaeagnus umbellata*) came to America from Afghanistan, and areas east to China and Japan. Today it's found from Maine to Virginia,

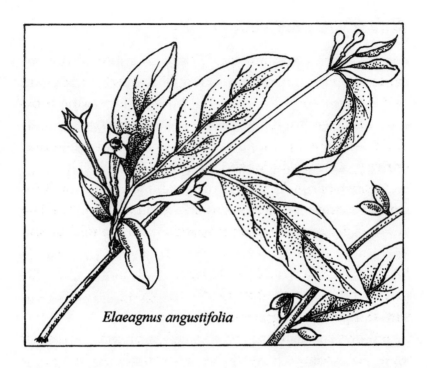

Elaeagnus angustifolia

then west to Wisconsin. It's a shrub that reaches a height
of some twenty feet, bearing very fragrant yellow flowers
and attractive red fruits in early fall. There are many
thorns on the branches.

Both species will easily take over native vegetation and
usurp valuable water. While the fruits are often cited as a
great bird food, it turns out that most native birds prefer
the fruits and berries of native plants.

Method of Removal: *Hand-pull seedlings as soon as you spot
their presence. With older plants, cut the trunks off at the base
and brush with a glyphosate herbicide.*

Burning Bush

Let's face it, when autumn comes around, the winged euonymus or burning bush (*Euonymus alatus*), is one breath-taking bush or small tree (up to twelve feet tall). As temperatures fall, the leaves become a brighter and more brilliant red (although some will amble toward shades of fuchsia), making this a statement specimen even when surrounded by other trees of great fall color.

Around 1860, the burning bush was introduced into America from northeastern Asia for use as an ornamental shrub. Because of that colorful fall display, highway departments and parkway planters across the Northeast adapted burning bush as a divider, in hedges, and as foundation plantings.

After the leaves fall, the gray-brown bark exposes the four corky wings that run up and down the twigs and branches, so even in winter, it has visual interest. Tiny, insignificant, four-petalled green flowers develop into elliptical scarlet red (sometimes off-purple) arils or berries. Each fruit contains four seeds. Birds love the seeds.

In urban conditions, growth seems to be checked but take it out to the woods and the fields, and it proliferates like mad. Again, burning bush not only crowds out native species in the woodlands of the Northeast but also easily spreads into fields and pastures, where the shade they produce affect sun-loving native wildflowers.

The invader is now common in Connecticut, New York, Pennsylvania, Virginia, and Illinois, and is moving south. It's quite common around the mountains of western North Carolina, especially along highways and backcountry roads.

Method of Removal: Seedlings can be pulled up, especially when in moist soil. Larger plants can be dug or pulled out with a weed wrench. The small trees can be cut at ground level, but should be ground down to prevent sprouts. You can also paint the cut stump with glyphosate.

Wintercreeper

Wintercreeper (*Euonymus fortunei*) is an evergreen climbing shrub. Its attractive foliage will amble along the ground, where it forms a dense understory, or climb trunks, fences, tree trunks, rocks, and even steps, using small roots that arise along the stems. Back in 1907, it was introduced into the States as an ornamental ground-cover.

When creeping, the plants are fairly benign, but like many of the ivies, when climbing trees or other vertical objects, they change their botanical structure. Clusters of inconspicuous green-white flowers appear on long stalks followed in the autumn by pinkish to red capsules. The capsules split open to expose seeds covered with a fleshy orange seed coat, or aril. Birds eat the seeds with relish.

If left unchecked, wintercreeper grows into a dense ground cover, smothering less powerful native plants and eventually leads to a lack of food and shelter for many animal species.

And don't forget that this particular *euonymus* is very susceptible to euonymus scale—just another reason for not introducing the species to home gardens.

Method of Removal: Pull up plants by hand but remember to get all of the roots because any little bit of root left has the ability to resprout. If infestations are beyond such control, try brushing a glyphosate herbicide to the cut stems.

English Holly

It's difficult to believe that such a time-honored plant as English holly (*Ilex aquifolium*) can cause trouble in native woodlands, but it can and it does.

The trees originally arrived in eastern American gardens around the 1700s, when they came over with settlers and gardeners. They reached the Pacific Northwest in the late 1800s. Not only have seedlings popped up throughout my own garden in Ashville, North Carolina, but this past winter while walking the Mountains to the Sea Trail just outside the city, I also found fairly mature specimens of English holly that obviously were seeded by birds who had picked up the seed in neighboring gardens.

It is a beautiful tree, often reaching heights of fifty feet. The bark is smooth and gray. Undulating evergreen leaves bear sharp spines, are dark green and waxy, and are especially attractive in the winter season. The flowers are small, greenish white, blooming in late spring. On female plants, clusters of red berries follow them. Berries remain on the branches for many months since birds only begin eating them near the end of the season.

It's difficult to talk out against a tree with such rich history—it is a symbol of Christmas for the Christians, and was even beloved by the Romans, who chose it as an icon for Saturnalia, their winter fest, beginning just before the new year.

Method of Removal: *Remove the seedling trees as soon as they are found. Since the roots and severed trunks do not sprout, a chainsaw is the choice for removing older trees.*

The Privets

The problem privets were often planted in hedges, massed in shrubberies, or used as specimen plants. There are three that have become pests: the Japanese privet (*Ligustrum japonicum*), the Chinese privet (*L. sinense*), and the common European privet (*L. vulgare*).

The common European privet probably came over to America as a hedge plant in the 1700s, when it began the process of naturalization (in later years it was replaced in the landscape by the evergreen shrub, *Ligustrum ovalifolium*). Japanese privet arrived just after World War II while the Chinese privet was introduced sometime in the mid-1950s.

Regardless of the species, the privets are easy to identify. Except for the evergreen (and more tender) Japanese privet, the other two are sometimes deciduous or evergreen according to the climate. All three have large, dark green, glossy leaves, and all have spring blossoms of white, often with a fragrance that some folks find appealing but others find offensive. And all three species produce persistent, black, berrylike fruits that often hang on the plants until the following spring.

The European and Chinese privets reach heights of about fifteen feet, while the Japanese can go to eighteen feet.

All are problem plants because they form dense, often impenetrable thickets that soon crowd out native plants. They spread not only by seed but also with suckers. In addition, when these privet thickets are invaded by Japanese honeysuckle or bittersweet, the problems escalate.

Method of Removal: *Seedlings can be pulled up by hand. Larger bushes can be cut off at ground level, and the stumps then brushed with a glyphosate herbicide.*

Bush Honeysuckle

There are currently three problem bush honeysuckles (but who knows what the future will hold?): the Amur honeysuckle (*Lonicera maackii*), the Morrow honeysuckle (*L. morrowii*), and the Tatarian honeysuckle (*L. tatarica*).

In general, the bush honeysuckles are deciduous shrubs from six to twenty-five feet tall. Elliptical leaves with short stems are opposite on the stems. Older stems are without pith and often hollow. In spring, depending on the species, pairs of very fragrant, tubular flowers of white (that often turn yellow with age) or pink appear at the leaf axils, followed by quarter-inch red to orange fruits.

The Amur, Morrow's, and Tartarian honeysuckle range from the central Great Plains to southern New England and south to Tennessee and North Carolina. Because they all originally came from Japan, China, Korea, Manchuria, Turkey, and southern Russia, they are usually cold hardy to USDA Zone 3.

Amur honeysuckle is the tallest of the group and with good soil and plenty of moisture can actually reach twenty-five feet in height. The white flowers yellow with age and the subsequent berries are glossy red. With age, this species gets unattractively rangy. A native of China and Japan, it was introduced to American back in 1986.

Morrow's honeysuckle came to the States in the late 1800s. This species has a dense growth habit, stays around six feet tall, has white flowers that yellow with age, and forms dark red berries.

Tartarian honeysuckles are natives of Turkey and were introduced back in the mid-1700s. Their height is about ten feet, and their flowers are usually white (again aging to yellow), but a number of escaped cultivars have flowers of varying hues.

These bushes produce abundant fruits, which can be any color between yellow and dark red. Indiscriminating birds eat them with relish. The Audubon Society reports that in the eastern United States, over twenty species feed on these persistent fruits and spread them all over. Yet, while the seeds have high sugar content, they lack the fats that our migratory birds need for long flights.

Because these shrubs are shade tolerant, they grow as undercover plants that easily block out the light that native plants need. In addition, bush honeysuckles usurp a great deal of the available water and, again, natives suffer.

You often find bush honeysuckles growing along the edges of woodlands, encroaching on abandoned fields and pastures. Along with miscanthus grasses and Japanese spiraea, backwoods roads not ten miles from my home are choked with these plants.

Method of Removal: *For such invasive plants, the bush honeysuckles have weak root systems, and can easily be pulled when small. Adult plants can be killed by cutting them down at ground level, then brushing the stumps with a glyphosate herbicide. In areas of great infestation, controlled burning has been suggested but with the continuing variations on rainfall across the United States this is probably not a safe solution.*

Japanese Knotweed

Although considered a bush, the Japanese knotweed (*Polygonum cuspidatum*) is really a herbaceous plant, which see under "Perennials."

Strawberry Guava

Although it is easy to forget exotic Hawaii is one of the United States, when it comes to weed invaders, along with mainland Florida and California, it seems to be a target center. The strawberry guava (*Psidium cattleianum*) is one of those invaders that is causing a great deal of havoc among the native plants of that region. In the early 1900s, it had been introduced into Hawaii for its edible fruit.

Strawberry guava, or purple guava, is a Brazilian shrub or small tree about fifteen feet in height at maturity. The trunk is smooth. The aromatic, two- to four-inch-long egg-shaped leaves are a shiny, dark-green, and arranged oppositely on the stem. Strawberry guava flowers are white with many stamens and the edible fruits resemble purple golf balls.

Today strawberry guava is only a serious threat in the six largest Hawaiian islands and southern Florida. There, like most exotics, it threatens native plants by forming light-robbing thickets and seems to be like a walnut, producing toxic chemicals that prevent other plants from taking root.

Method of Removal: *Strawberry guava spreads by root sprouts and seed that is distributed chiefly by feral pigs and some birds. One of the best ways to control strawberry guava is to control the spread of feral pigs. This is followed by cutting. There is some evidence that applications of a glyphosate herbicide are an effective control.*

Buckthorn

A shrub or a small tree, the common or European buck-thorn (*Rhamnus cathartica*), ranges between a petite six feet up to a strapping twenty-five feet in height, and has a trunk up to ten inches wide. The common names refer to the sharp thorns growing at the branch tips. Plants were introduced from Eurasia as possible windbreaks and fence-rows during the 1800s. It should be noted that we have native buckthorns that are easily confused with the exotic species.

Its bark is gray to brown and rough when mature. When cut, the inner bark is yellow. Leaves are oval, rounded, or pointed at the tip, and have toothed margins, remaining green long after most leaves have turned color and fallen.

In spring, clusters of two to six yellow-green, four-petalled flowers appear, with male and female flowers on separate plants. Abundant quarter-inch purple-black fruits appear in late summer, each containing three to four seeds. Today these shrubs have naturalized from Nova Scotia, south to Missouri and east to New England. They are invasive threats that displace native species and are not too fussy as to habitat, adapting to open fields, the edge of woodlands, and even along roadsides. Buckthorn is also an alternate host of the crown "rust" of oats, which affects oat yield and quality.

Also note that all parts of these plants contain a chemical called anthraquinones, and cause vomiting and diarrhea if eaten. When birds eat the seeds, they, too, get diarrhea, thus helping to distribute plants far and wide.

Method of Removal: *Seedlings are easily removed by hand. Saplings and older shrubs can be cut but resprouting can occur. These can be brushed with a glyphosate herbicide.*

Multiflora Rose

Everybody loves a rose, right? Well, not *all* roses are beloved. The Japanese multiflora rose (*Rosa multiflora*) is one of these pariahs. Introduced into gardens in 1875, the plants came from Japan and Korea. It was widely promoted from the 1930s to the 1970s by conservation agencies and commercial nurseries for wildlife cover and wildlife food, as well as "living fences" to divide properties, which, according to old nursery advertisements kept close neighbors, good friends.

These are erect shrubs, often up to ten feet tall, with gracefully arching stems (all armed with spines), forming dense, usually impenetrable thickets.

In May, branches are covered with one-inch wide fragrant white, red, or pink blossoms, centered with golden yellow stamens, followed in late summer to fall by oval red hips, about a quarter-inch in diameter.

So what's wrong? Well, this rose is just another example of a plant that behaves itself when growing on its home turf but becomes an obnoxious thug when traveling abroad.

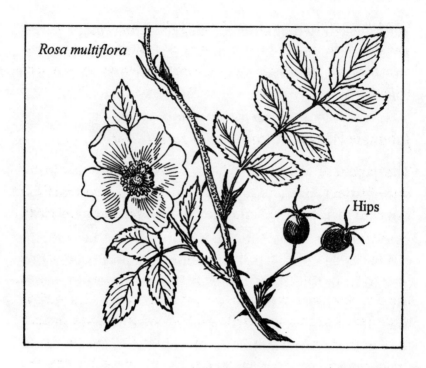

Rosa multiflora

Hips

I have walked back trails in the Great Smoky Mountains, often many miles from any civilization, and there
along the trail were multiflora roses, growing in abundance. These plants are now classified as noxious weeds in
Iowa and New Jersey, and should be called pests across the
Northeast. When I gardened in western Sullivan County,
some 125 miles north of New York City, I saw field after
field full of these roses. There, it would disrupt beautiful
native plants such as the lovely pasture rose (*Rosa carolina*).
And, take note, they are heading south to Alabama and
Georgia.

Method of Removal: *Immediately pull up seedlings as soon as you spot them. Use a brush hog to mow down thorny tops, and then treat the stumps with a glyphosate herbicide, as they will resprout.*

Japanese Wineberry and Himalayan Raspberry

The Japanese wineberry (*Rubus phoenicolasius*) was introduced from China and Japan as a food crop, first reaching England in about 1876 and then the United States in 1890, imported by John Lewis Childs.

Plants are grown for their silvery foliage and their edible red fruits. The canes are long and recurving, rooting at the tip. They bear weak but nearly straight prickles and an abundance of red-brown glandular hairs that look beautiful when sprinkled with dew. Their height can be up to nine feet with a nine-foot spread. Their small flowers are white or sometimes tinged with a pink cast. Developing fruits are enclosed by the flowers' sepals, making them look like Japanese lanterns, until ripe. The plants are very hardy.

The wineberry has escaped from cultivation and is now a problem in USDA Zones 6 and 7. If not kept under control, the plant easily spreads with its tip-rooting habit. The result is an impenetrable thicket that crowds out both native plants and wildlife. This crowding can be kept somewhat at bay, by growing the canes on supports so the tips cannot root. Plants can also spread by seed.

Plant breeders crossed this species with *Rubus idaeus,* the red raspberry. When the species is crossed, yellow-fruits are produced.

Himalayan raspberries (*Rubus ellipticus*) hail from southern Asia and tropical China. They were introduced into Hawaii as both a fruit plant and an ornamental.

Plants are stout evergreen shrubs with prickly canes, growing about twelve feet long. Flowers are white, blooming in short terminal branches. The fruit is yellow and reportedly delicious.

Like their Japanese relatives, these plants proliferate into barrier thickets, displacing native plants and animals. To date, they're only a problem in Hawaii.

Method of Removal: *Prevent wineberries from spreading by growing the canes on supports so the tips cannot root. Plants also spread by seed. Because these are foodstuffs, the safest control is to cut the plants back to the ground using a mower or, wearing gloves, using a hand-held weeder. Continue to cut off any new growth.*

Brazilian Pepper Tree

In 1891, the Brazilian pepper tree (*Schinus terebinthifolius*), a native of Argentina, Paraguay, and Brazil, was introduced into the Florida scene as an ornamental. It is an aggressive plant and today it's found in southern Arizona, southern California, Texas, and Louisiana. Tens of thousands of acres have fallen prey to this plant.

Beginning as an attractive tropical shrub (or small tree), the Brazilian pepper tree usually stands between ten and fifteen feet tall. Its pinnate or featherlike leaves (somewhat resembling sumacs), bear leaflets having a red midrib that grow from a red stem. When crushed, the leaves smell of turpentine. Small white flowers develop into clusters of glossy green berries that turn bright red. The red skin dries to become a papery shell surrounding the seed. The fruit ripens toward the end of the year. According to the Audubon Society, a number of birds chow down on the seeds, including robins, who consider the seeds a favorite food. Other animals also eat the fruits.

Related to poison ivy, the plants can cause contact dermatitis. Although the fruits are often sold as gourmet foods, sensitive people should avoid eating them.

The pepper tree grows in moist soils, and is especially fond of stream and canal banks. It is an invader and destroyer of native plant habitats where it forms a dense canopy that shades out natural vegetation. Nonetheless, like many other exotics, it is still being sold as an ornamental tree.

Method of Removal: *Seedlings and small saplings can be pulled up by hand, but remember to wear gloves. All roots must be removed or they will resprout. A triclopyr herbicide can be applied to the bark about a foot off the ground. Bush hogs are effective in removal.*

Japanese Spiraea

We all seem to have feet of clay and until I walked some of the back woods around Asheville, North Carolina, where I

Spiraea japonica

live, I had no idea just how invasive Japanese spiraea was. Why even the JC Raulston Arboretum in Raleigh had the species included in their plant distribution back in 1999. Today, they no longer do. It's a shame that such a beautiful bush is such a deadly enemy to many native plants, especially in my area of the Southeast.

Around 1870, Japanese spiraea (*Spiraea japonica*) was introduced into the Northeast from Japan, Korea, and China through the good offices of a number of nurseries who thought they were dealing with an excellent landscape plant.

It's a perennial, deciduous shrub in the rose family that usually grows between five and six feet tall. Three-inch egg-shaped leaves alternate along graceful reddish-brown stems. In midsummer clusters of very pretty, very small, rosy pink flowers bloom in flat-topped inflorescences (actually several clusters that are close together) up to three inches wide. There are many cultivars available today.

Japanese spiraea is a rapid grower and with plentiful seed, a rampant spreader, and will do well in either sun or shade. Hundreds of tiny seeds are distributed by animals, hikers, and by runoff from rain. Once fallen into a stream, seeds will be carried by water to new pastures.

It's especially fond of settling into wooded pathways or rooting by the edges of backcountry roads or invading the land along streams and riverbanks. Once established, it forms dense colonies that are almost impenetrable, not only to hikers but to animals, too. The seeds can remain in the soil for years before sprouting. Thanks to its profile nature, this shrub has now naturalized throughout much of the Northeast, Southeast, and Midwest.

Method of Removal: In small areas, cut the individual bushes to the ground remembering to do it before flowering and seed development. On larger plantings use a brush hog. Re-cutting is necessary because the roots resprout. Applications of a glyphosate herbicide may be necessary.

Guelder Rose

The Guelder rose (*Viburnum opulus* var. *opulus*) looks like the common elder so it's sometimes called the red elder or rose elder. It's a deciduous shrub growing about twelve feet tall, bearing toothed, maplelike leaves. The name Guelder comes from Gueldersland, a Dutch province where the trees were originally cultivated. They were introduced to America from Eurasia in the latter part of the seventeenth century.

These shrubs bloom with conspicuous, three- to five-inch-wide, nearly flat-topped heads of snow-white flowers. The inner blossoms are small and fertile and are surrounded by an outer ring of large, showy, sterile blossoms. Only the inner flowers result in fruits, which form drooping clusters of bright red berries, usually in August. The berries are bitter and have a somewhat disagreeable odor—although birds love them. At one time the berries were said to be poisonous but that warning seems to have been overstated.

The Guelder rose is another shrub that knows no bounds. Because it's highly adaptable to soil conditions, it invades wildly divergent areas where it chokes out native plants. There are fears it might interbreed with the native highbush cranberry (*Viburnum opulus* var. *trilobum*), giving rise to a truly invasive monster.

Method of Removal: *Pull up seedlings by hand. Once the root system develops, shrubs must be cut off at ground level. Then brush the stumps with a glyphosate herbicide to prevent resprouting.*

9

Grasses, Sedges, and Bamboo

Many weedy grasses have two characteristics that help in spreading their bad habits: They are wind-pollinated and they have tenacious and spreading roots. While representing the most important single plant family on earth, which alone produces all the cereal grains that have sustained humanity throughout recorded history, their rampant growth habits often turn a friend into a decided foe.

Grasses are unique in their pollination. Instead of having colorful petals or attractive floral parts, the flowers of grasses have very small petals, sometimes needing a magnifying glass to be seen. The flowers exchanged pollination by insects for dependence on the wind for pollen transferrence and often (but not always) seed distribution.

Exotic grasses are adept at taking over abandoned farmland and provide serious competition to valuable crop and native plants across the country. The following are the worst offenders.

European Beach Grass

Because of their ability to act as sand-binding grasses, European beach grass (*Ammophila arenaria*), like its American counterpart *A. breviligulata*, belong to a genus of very important grasses.

The European variety was introduced in the early 1900s to the vicinity of San Francisco to act as a sand binder and has now, unfortunately, established itself as a threat to the dunes along the Pacific coastline.

Ammophila arenaria is a tough, coarse, erect perennial grass that grows in small tufts, the tufts connected by an extensive network of creeping rhizomes. Flowering occurs from May to August and consists of a pale tan cylindrical, spike-like panicle, up to a foot long. The seeds suffer from the environment and the plants usually spread by the rhizomes.

Ammophila arenaria threatens coastal sand dunes by displacing native dune species, thus changing the entire ecology of a dune. Coastal sand dunes around the world are under siege as a result of European beach grass taking root. Because of its tough rhizomes, it easily shoves out native plants, and in so doing, changes the very blueprint of what makes successful dune ecology.

The spread of *A. arenaria* can be controlled through manual removal, but this type of control requires ongoing treatment. Control should be emphasized until eradication techniques are refined. Further research is a high priority and is currently being carried out by Humboldt State University, California.

Method of Removal: *Manual removal (digging) controls the spread of* A. arenaria *but is labor intensive. In one case, complete removal was achieved, but the site was subsequently invaded by other exotic species. In the first year, monthly treatment intervals are suggested; in subsequent years, frequency can be decreased. Monitoring should be conducted to determine if exotic species, such as* Carpobrotus, *are replacing* A. arenaria. *Ultimately, revegetation with native species should be a standard part of management, once control techniques are refined.*

Giant Reed Grass

The giant reed grass (*Arundo donax*) originally came from India and was probably introduced into California back in the early 1800s.

There are a number of products derived from this grass. Reeds for clarinets, bassoons, and oboes are all crafted from cut pieces of its culms, as once were the pipes for primitive pipe organs. Like bamboos, giant reed stems are used as fishing rods, and their cut sections are also employed in basketry.

Known in California as wild cane, this is a very tall, perennial grass that can easily reach a height of thirty feet,

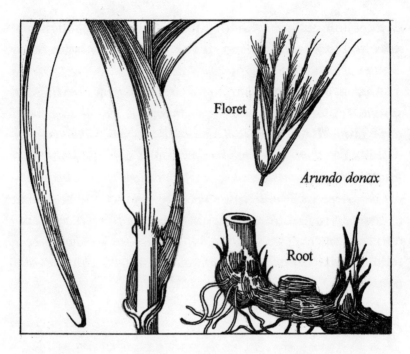

Floret

Arundo donax

Root

with a tough root system that reaches deeply into the soil. Its leaves are up to two inches wide and a foot long, with flowers borne in dense, plumelike panicles often two feet long. They bloom in late summer.

In addition to aesthetic purposes, giant reed grasses were once used as windbreaks, and as was *Spartina*, another native prairie grass, as thatching for sod houses. But it was its use as an erosion controller in areas threatened by annual flooding that led it to become an invasive plant.

Giant reed can grow into dense hummocks of gigantic culms that offer nothing to wildlife, except holding mud in check. When dried, the culms become major fire hazards. Their speedy growth crowds out native plants, and can change the directions of streams. In addition, pieces of this grass can float on floodwaters where they eventually jam up drainage outlets. Some of the fragments can root and start new grass stands.

Today, it's found in USDA Zone 7 and warmer, from California over to Arkansas and on to Virginia and Kentucky.

I've had a variegated form in my garden for years. Because of the lack of some chlorophyll in these green and white cultivars, growth is held in check. Although floral plumes are produced in the fall, I've never found viable seeds and most authorities assume that propagation is only through vegetative means.

Method of Removal: While areas of heavy infestations are best controlled with glyphosate herbicides, smaller patches can be defeated with continued mowing. Remember, if pulled out of the ground, even the smallest bit of root can start a new plant.

The Brome Grasses

There are a number of weedy brome grasses that cause trouble in the United States. The following rank high on the list: Hungarian brome or awnless brome (*Bromus inermis*); Japanese brome (*Bromus japonicus*); and foxtail brome (*Bromus rubens*).

Hungarian or awnless brome (*Bromus sterilis*) is a deeply rooted, rhizomatous perennial grass, distinguished by the lack of an awn (a bristlelike appendage that extends from a grass flower).

These grasses, which were introduced into the United States back in the late 1800s, are cool season exotics that invade old fields and pastures. In its native Europe, smooth brome is found along roadsides, riverbanks, and the edges of fields, woods, and pastures. Today, they range from the northern Great Plains, down to Tennessee and also from California to Alaska.

Method of Removal: The best way to control this grass is by cutting the plants before they go to seed. There are effective chemical means but they are generally outside of the experience of the homeowner and advice should be sought from local extension agents.

Japanese brome (*Bromus japonicus*) is an annual grass reaching a height of a little under three feet. Both its stems and its blades are covered with soft hairs. The flowers bloom in a panicle with individual spikelets about a half-inch long, borne on long, drooping stalks.

This grass is a weed of grain fields, pastures, and abandoned land, introduced into America sometime in the mid-1900s. It's found in every state of the union and is termed a noxious weed because of competition with native grasses and wildflowers. It's especially prevalent in acid soils.

Method of Removal: The best way to control this grass is by cutting the plants before they go to seed. There are effective chemical means but they are generally outside of the experience of the homeowner and advice should be sought from local extension agents.

Foxtail brome (*Bromus rubens*) is another annual brome grass, growing about two feet high, and easily spotted by its floral panicle, densely packed with seeds, having a decided purplish tinge, and a close resemblance to its namesake.

The seeds arrived from Europe sometime in the mid-1800s as an unplanned-for weed. The seeds are stiff and sharp, and are a threat to animals and birds, often lodging in the animal's eye. Today it's found primarily in the West but has moved as far east as Massachusetts. Like many invasive grasses, it's tolerant of most poor but disturbed soil.

Method of Removal: Because foxtail bromes are shallow-rooted plants, they can easily be pulled up by hand. Remove them before they go to seed.

Pampas Grass and Andean Pampas Grass

The plumes of pampas grass (*Cortaderia selloana*) and Andean pampas grass (*C. jubata*) have long been favorites of the horticultural trade; nonetheless, the first grass is a problem on the West Coast and in the Southeast. Jubata grass, up to now, is invasive only out West. Both species are natives of South America; pampas grass entering California back in 1848, where nurserymen imported plants from Argentina and Jubata grass arriving in the early 1900s.

In the Southeast, pampas grass has become a landscaping cliché; it's the ornamental grass that is planted on either side of the pillars marking driveways back to count-less motels and tourist homes. In English gardens, pampas grasses have long reigned supreme for the sheer size and beauty of their flowering plumes.

Both of these grasses are called tussock grasses, growing in large clumps of graceful leaves. They do well along ditches and roadsides, and are quick to settle in bare and re-cently disturbed earth. The two species are quite similar; but their difference lies in their plumes: Jubata grass bears its brownish purple flowers on stems that stand well above the fountain of leaves; on pampas grass, the silvery white to pink plumes (according to the cultivar described), stand only a bit above the leaves. Once encamped, both species easily crowd out native plants and when dry, can easily catch fire.

Jubata grass is called apomictic, which means that the flowers produce millions of seeds that develop without pollination. Blown about by the wind, they fall to earth miles from the parent plant, quickly germinating on al-most any kind of soil. In California, you'll often find peo-ple who stop on the roadside, pick the plumes, and while waving them about, send viable seed out on the four winds. Pampas grass is a bit less lethal since both male and female parts are necessary for seeds to appear.

Method or Removal: *The seedlings grow quickly and soon de-velop the kind of root system that is nearly impossible to pull out by hand so pulling must be done when they are very young. In order to make sure that herbicides do the job, remove as many grass blades as possible before applications of a glyphosate herbicide.*

Chufa or Yellow Nut-grass

This is one of those rare occasions when I must blast a plant as being a weed, knowing that in many respects it has paid its dues to humanity—and, who knows, eventually it might be forced to do it again. A native of both North America and Eurasia, chufa is usually included in the Five Worst Weeds in the U.S. list.

Chufa or yellow nut-grass (*Cyperus esculentus*) is considered to be a weed in today's world but for centuries it's been used as an edible tuber with common names like edible galingale, earth-almond, coco sedge, and rush-nut.

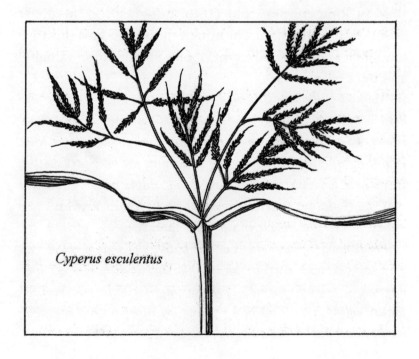

Cyperus esculentus

The nuts are reputed to taste similar to almonds and can be eaten raw or cooked. Recipes abound.

The plant is perennial with slender rhizomes ending in nearly round tubers. Like all sedges and rushes, the stem is triangular in cross section. Height is about three feet or slightly under with narrow light green leaves and numerous flat spikelets, usually a straw color or yellowish brown.

This is a weed of wetlands, ditches, pond margins, and streams, in addition to spring wetlands and waste areas in general. It also infects turf grass in golf courses, lawns, and parks. Remember, each of the below-ground tubers can generate a new plant.

Most homeowners object to nut-grass on aesthetic grounds, but the plants, although native, do have invasive tendencies and usually crowd out much more valuable and needed species.

Method of Removal: Unlike the majority of lawn weeds, chufa does not respond to the usual chemicals employed by the homeowner. The best way to remove this plant from your home grounds is pulling up by hand, beginning as soon as the foliage is spotted. If you wait too long, the rhizomes begin to dig in and it's doubtful that you'll pull up the entire root system. Every few weeks it's necessary to check the area again for new sprouts.

For removal of large areas of this plant, you should check with your local extension service because the chemicals needed are usually not within the purview of the average homeowner. Never use plants collected near working farms because various chemicals might have already poisoned them.

Crabgrass

Crabgrass (*Digitaria* spp.) is one of those monster lawn weeds that can get any lawn lover ranting and raving, then quietly sobbing. Also know as finger grass, it's one of some 300 species of grasses that began their careers in Europe and Asia then were introduced into the United States where they have naturalized with a vengeance.

Their particular talent lies in their stems, which upon hitting the earth will root at a joint. Even though they are annuals, and go through their entire life cycle in one summer, their ease of rooting makes their eradication difficult.

The seeds will overwinter in the ground and germinate in the late spring after many other weeds have already started their yearly attacks.

Large crabgrass (*D. sanguinalis*) has stout stems that are often up to three feet long. Its preferred position is prostrate on the ground and, of course, it also roots at the joints. Hairy leaf blades are usually one-third of an inch wide with the leaf sheaths also sprouting hairs. The flowers appear in ten long segments whirling about the tip of the stem, like thin fingers from a thin wrist. Small seeds are plentiful. This grass is at home in fields, gardens, and lawns, and it is especially troublesome in the South.

Smooth crabgrass (*D. ischaemum*) is similar to the above but not as coarse or as tall, having no hairs, and is at home in most lawns throughout the United States.

Keep in mind that if you put in the effort to maintain a lawn, it must be well watered, properly fertilized, and full of grass roots to keep weeds like crabgrass from invading. Never cut your grass too short because keeping the blades reasonably long keeps soil cool, thus preventing the germination of seeds.

Once crabgrass is on the scene, it's especially important to follow the suggestions cited above. Following the regime keeps crabgrass from developing the dense growth that smothers the best part of your lawn.

Method of Removal: *In addition to following the previous advice to control crabgrass, fertilize your lawn, then keep the cutting edge of your lawnmower at three to four inches. Once the crabgrass is gone, you can lower the cutting height to two inches. You can also buy a crabgrass control at your local nursery center. Zap small infestations with a glyphosate herbicide.*

Goosegrass

Goosegrass or wiregrass (*Eleusine indica*) is another annual member of the grass family that has long been a great public enemy of lawn lovers.

This threat is an annual that grows flat on the ground. Branching at the base, the stems are very smooth and very prostrate. They resemble a rosette or silvery mat. The leaves are dark green, hairy near the base, about a foot long, and usually flat. Flower stems are short and compressed, consisting of two to ten flattened fingerlike spikes that look like a zipper. Seed heads are somewhat similar to those of crabgrass but shorter and stiff.

Unlike the kind of turf you want, goosegrass is usually at home where the earth has been subjected to heavy use. Reproduction is by seed that germinates a few weeks after crabgrass hits the scene. Root systems are fibrous.

Method of Removal: Pull up or dig out any goosegrass that you see using a narrow-pointed digger. Then be sure you follow the same regime as suggested for crabgrass.

Tall Fescue

Tall fescue (*Festuca arundinacea*), sometimes called Kentucky fescue, is a long-lived perennial grass and a native of Europe, often planted in the United States as both a forage grass and a lawn grass. Today it's found from Florida west to Texas, and north to Canada.

The leaf blades are thick and coarse, growing from a basal clump and can reach a height of four or five feet. The stems (or culms) are hollow with the leaves enclosed by the leaf sheath collar. The flowering, open panicles are from three to ten inches long. The panicles have a slightly purplish cast.

The grass is considered a mixed blessing because when grown under controlled conditions, it's a valuable forage crop. But left unattended, it becomes a major pest.

Once again, in many of our American prairies, this fescue has turned invasive, crowding out the native species. It invades grasslands, open woodlands, and marshy areas. In addition, many of the plants are infected with an endophytic fungus, a fancy word that means a plant growing upon or within a plant. Known as *Neotyphodium coenophialum,* this fungus manufactures toxic alkaloids, that not only cause the plant to be obnoxious to its non-species neighbors, but are also able to make herbivores ill. Symptoms include induced abortions in mares, reduced fertility in small mammals, and a gangrenous condition called fescue foot.

The worst part of this disease is its reproductive process. It does not spread by spores, but the fungus remains in seed heads and goes from one plant generation to the next, being able to survive over a year. All parts of the plant can be infected.

Method of Removal: *Glyphosate herbicides can be applied in the late fall when other species are dormant.*

Cogon Grass

Cogon grass (*Imperata cylindrica*) has the distinction of being one of the top ten weed pests in the world. Some lists rank it as high as number seven.

It's a grass native to southeast Asia, China, and Japan that was introduced into the United States both by design and by accident. In the first instance, back in the 1930s, the grass was distributed by the USDA as a forage grass (for which it's almost useless) and for soil erosion (which it does with a bang). In the second instance, cogon grass arrived on our shores as packing material (another species of *Imperata* is used to make paper).

Cogon grass is an aggressive perennial that grows up to four feet in height. The leaves are about an inch wide and have a prominent white midrib, ending in a sharp point. Silvery flowers blossom in a cylindrical panicle up to a foot long and less than two inches wide. Because the finely toothed leaf margins contain silica crystals, it's not useful as a forage grass.

An attractive cultivar of cogon grass known as 'Red Baron' has also been marketed for years by the nursery trade for the red color displayed by the top half of the blades.

An erect perennial grass that spreads by seed and by invasive rhizomes, cogon grass is found throughout the South and as far west as Texas. It's also been reported growing in Oregon.

This grass is an invasive, with an ability to overtake existing ecosystems by forming a tightly packed thatch that stifles the growth of other plants. Not only native plants, but also many kinds of wildlife are at risk when cogon grass makes any headway into an environment. Remember, it is tolerant of most soil types, from sand to clay, and will withstand salinity and nearby water.

There is also a fear that the cultivar 'Red Baron' could hybridize with the species, creating an even more dangerous plant because the cultivar is hardy into USDA Zone 6.

If any 'Red Baron' blood grass grows in your garden, be sure to watch for plants that revert to the species.

Method of Removal: *Small patches can be dug up or repeatedly mowed. Large infestations should be plowed as deeply as possible, and regrowth treated with a glyphosate herbicide.*

Japanese Stilt Grass

If Shakespeare had known Japanese stilt grass, I'm sure he might have written: "What charming leaf with its off-centered vein has taken over my hollow?" But fortunately for Shakespeare these weeds had not yet left Asia when he started to garden. This twentieth-century addition to America's world of weeds would be prized as a plant for shady places, if it knew when to stop. But it doesn't.

Japanese stilt grass (*Microstegium vimineum*, formerly *Eulalia vimineum*) is also known as Asian stilt grass, Vietnamese stilt grass, Nepal microstegium, Nepalese brown-top, and Chinese packing grass. The scientific name is from the Greek *micros*, small, and *stege*, to cover, referring to the seed structure.

It was probably introduced into Tennessee just after the end of the First World War when it was used to pack porcelain imported from China. Since then, it has spread to all states east of the Mississippi, from Connecticut and southward.

Stilt grass is an annual forming dense mats over the summer. The usually reclining stems reach a length of about forty inches and often root at the stem nodes. The lime green leaves, four to five inches in length and half an inch wide, taper at both ends and have a silvery stripe of reflective hairs down the middle of their upper surface. The leaves are unusual because the white midvein doesn't divide a leaf in half; the leaf surface on one side of the vein is always larger than the other.

Japanese stilt grass prefers moist soils that are shaded from full sun. That habitat preference points to another botanical oddity of this grass: It has a great ability to conduct photosynthesis even when the leaves must depend on flecks of light—the kind of light found in woodlands where trees dapple the sunlight as the sun passes across the summer sky.

Look for this grass in ditches, in marshes, wooded hollows, drained floodplains, woodland borders, damp meadows, woodland thickets, lawns, and along streams and roadsides. Wet soils that experience periods of standing water are shunned although the seeds can survive and germinate after extended periods in this environment. Studies show that a stilt grass seed can stay viable for at least three years and is another seed belonging to the group known as "seeds of the troubled earth."

Method of Removal: *The best strategy for controlling Japanese stilt grass is pulling up hanks of the grass by hand, before plants form seed. Glyphosate herbicides are effective but remember, they are not specific as to what they kill. Being an annual, stilt grass cut late in the late summer will die back for the winter.*

Chinese Silver Grass or Eulalia Grass

I've watched Chinese silver grass *(Miscanthus sinensis [M. japonica])* invade vast areas of western North Carolina, beginning in the late 1970s. As the result of an extensive drought, bales of hay were shipped east from neighboring states; wrapped within those bales were the seeds heads of this grass.

A native of eastern Asia, silver grass arrived on our shores toward the end of the 1850s, when it was very popular in Victorian-style ornamental grass gardens. This species was often the choice for landscaping zoos and public parks, for building windscreens, and for hiding unpleasant objects from view.

Silver grass is a hardy perennial, very robust in habit, growing in clumps that get larger, year after year, reaching from six to nine feet in height. The deep green leaves are more than an inch wide, with a prominent white stripe down the center of each leaf; they are from two to three feet long. Flowers are brownish, silky, and bloom in plume-like panicles that are very showy in early to late autumn. They have always been described (and often the fact is ignored) as heavy seeders, the wind blowing the seeds in all directions.

Today the plants are found throughout the eastern and southern United States, west to Texas. Here in North Carolina they are spotted along all the interstate highways.

It is assumed that all cultivars of this species are sterile and in all my wanderings, I've never found a seedling with the characteristics of the major horticultural choices, 'Zebrinus,' 'Gracillimus,' and 'Variegatus.'

Method of Removal: Donning gloves and using a pruning saw or sharp pruners, cut the grass as close to the ground as possible, making sure you start before the plants go to seed. Use a glyphosate herbicide on the remaining clump. Unless you live by yourself in the middle of an wide-open area, do not do what old garden books suggest and burn the clumps of grass.

Fountain grass

Crimson fountain grass (*Pennisetum setaceum*) is one of the more popular varieties of ornamental grasses usually touted as "special" for all American gardens. These plants do resemble fountains with their showy foxtail-like plumes that bloom in early summer. The long, narrow, purplish pink flower heads rise above neat symmetrical mounds of grassy foliage between two and three feet high. They are natives of Northern Africa.

These grasses are not a major problem in areas with harsh winters because they cease perennial growth north of USDA Zone 7. But woe is the gardener in warmer climes, for this particular fountain grass is a highly aggressive colonizer that easily out-competes native plants. It can even rapidly reestablish its turf after a fire sweeps through.

In Hawaii, fountain grass is a major threat to many imperiled native plant species, which are some of the most closely knit plant communities in the world. But it's also running rampant in Arizona, California, and Colorado. In Southern California, fountain grass invades grasslands and canyons, where in the dry seasons, a carelessly tossed cigarette can devastate entire communities.

In warmer areas, fountain grass is a perennial that uses the wind to spread seed. The seeds can remain viable in the soil for six years or longer. The seeds also stick to the coats of animals, the mud on cars and trucks, and the pants and boots of humans.

Method of Removal: Small infestations can be removed by uprooting clumps after a rainfall when the earth is friable. But always remember to remove the ripening inflorescences in order to prevent seed dispersal. Because the seeds lasts so long, hand removal may be necessary a number of times in one year.

Annual Bluegrass

Annual bluegrass *(Poa annua)* is a major pest in the United States, a weed first introduced from South America. Large expanses of it are usually found in lawns from mid- to late-spring, when short seed heads form at the same level at which the lawn is mowed. It also thrives in the winter in the warmer parts of the country.

There are two varieties of annual bluegrass found in the South: The first is a plant with an upright and clumping

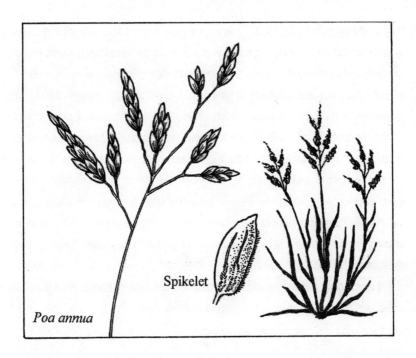

Spikelet

Poa annua

growth habit, and the second is a variety that creeps upon the ground. The upright form is an annual and produces an abundance of seed. The decumbent variety is a perennial, produces little seed, and dies back during the heat of the summer. The leaves are a bright green, usually eight to ten inches tall, with flattened stems (or culms) and loose panicles of small seeds.

This weedy grass is found found from Newfoundland to Alaska, and south to Florida and California in open ground, lawns, pastures, waste places, wooded clearings, and to the great chagrin of golf clubs, it's a pernicious weed of golfing turf. It's another grass that hates to grow surrounded by other grasses so it's at its best in areas that are closely mowed, such as lawns and golf courses. Because seeds germinate through most of the year, chemical controls are not always practical.

Be warned: This is one of the few plants known to science that can produce viable seed just twenty-four hours (give or take one or two) after pollination! It's about the only species that actually over-seeds itself as you mow.

Method of Removal: *The best way to control annual bluegrass is with a pre-emergent or a post-emergent herbicide but, because either of these are not the average chemical found over the counter, it's suggested that you contact your local extension agent to see what's new in the annual bluegrass herbicide bin.*

Yellow Foxtail

Yellow foxtail or yellow bristlegrass *(Setaria lutescens [S. glauca])* is a warm season annual grass with blossoms of some beauty, although the plant itself is not elegant enough to maintain in lawn or garden.

You can't miss yellow foxtail. It grows as a coarse, upright bunch-type grass about four feet tall. The leaves are flat and smooth. The flowers are cylindrical spikes from two to five inches long, bristly and dense (leading to closely packed seeds) and looking exactly like their common name.

Method of Removal: Since these grasses are shallow rooted, the easiest way to maintain control of its spread is to pull up plants by hand. You can also keep them cut close to the ground, thus preventing seeding.

Johnson Grass

Johnson grass or sorghum *(Sorghum halapense)* is another weed grass high on the list of undesirable plants. I've seen it continue to spread along the interstates in the Southeast, and recently find its way to the back roads.

Back in the 1840s, William Johnson introduced this Mediterranean native to America, when he imported the seeds as a potentially valuable hay crop. Unfortunately, it proved to be a noxious weed. The leaves can be poisonous to cattle and the frozen leaves are often fatal, too.

Johnson grass grows in dense clumps and reaches a height of about eight feet. The long, graceful blades have a pronounced white midvein while the stems themselves are usually a light shade of red toward the base of the clump. The flower heads are large and loosely branched, covered with reddish-brown seeds.

It's found in open fields, ditches, abandoned pastures, waste places, and along stream banks, from Massachusetts to Kansas, then south to Florida and Texas—in fact, just about everywhere east of the Mississippi and is actively spreading west.

The grass is an aggressive spreader, easily crowding out native species, and lacks any qualities that wildlife would find attractive.

Method of Removal: *This is one pernicious weed! Small areas of Johnson grass can be brought under control by pulling out seedlings and young plants when the earth is moist. A glyphosate herbicide can be applied to the leaves of mowed plants toward the end of the summer.*

Reed Canary Grass

I was first introduced to reed canary grass (*Phalaris arundinacea*) when visiting an upstate New York landfill. There the grass grew in profusion because people in the area had emptied birdcages, then tossed the garbage out at the dump. There, the uneaten birdseed germinated.

The grass is found from southern Alaska to the eastern Atlantic, then south to Kentucky, all the way down to Arkansas. It also has a strong foothold out West.

Reed canary is a perennial grass with creeping rhizomes and erect culms, which can reach a height of three to six feet. Leaf blades are flat. The flowers appear in dense, branched panicles up to six inches long, and packed with seeds. It is not to be confused with a variegated form with white stripes that is grown as an ornamental grass called "ribbon grass" or as the English term the plant, "gardener's gators" (*Phalaris arundinacea* var. *picta*).

Not only will this grass invade landfills, it also has a penchant for irrigation ditches and small streams, where it quickly becomes a dominant plant. Except for some canaries, it's not an acceptable food for wildlife.

Method of Removal: With small areas of infestation, you can easily pull up the offending plants by hand. For larger plantings, try mowing before the seed forms, then covering the offending area with black plastic to bake the roots. Because the plants are often found around water, you should only use a glyphosate herbicide under the strictest of controls.

Common Reed Grass

Called common reed grass in northern New Jersey, *Phragmites autstralis* is a spectacularly tall perennial grass found on all continents except Antarctica.

This grass has been used for centuries as a material to thatch roofs, weave mattings, and even make rafts. Although in home and byway environments, it's viewed as a flagrant weed, in the bays and inlets around New York City and New Jersey, it's an important member of the ecosystem.

You can't miss it. Stems rise up to a height of fourteen feet and in late summer are topped by beautiful drooping, feathery collections of hundreds of tiny flowers that wave like Egyptian plumes in the wind.

Common reed is known as a colonial plant that spreads by its rhizomes. It forms huge stands, sometimes in ditches, sometimes in marshes, and often in the brackish water found where fresh-water and sea water systems overlap.

Arguments are now raging over attempts to remove these grasses. After all, if they disappeared from the New Jersey swamplands, what would hold it all together? Yet, on a local level, if you're being invaded by these grasses, you obviously must do something to combat them.

Method of Removal: *The best way to control them is to cut them back as close to the earth as possible, and then apply a glyphosate herbicide.*

Bamboos

Bamboos fall into two categories: those that clump and those that creep. The creepers are usually the bad guys in any home or garden setting, and the clumpers are more demure and conservative in their growth habits.

Running bamboos of any species send out far-reaching rhizomes that will go over (or under) most any obstacle in their endless pursuit of *lebensraum,* the space to live and grow. They give the word invasive new meaning, and unless you restrict their growth before or as you plant them, you will soon confront an out-of-control jungle.

One method of control is to plant them in steel drums, the kind that shippers use, completely sinking the drums in the ground.

Another method is to use barriers of concrete or sheet metal that are at least forty inches high. Planting them at the edges of driveways or sidewalks often works to contain them but even then, their searching rhizomes often find a way under the barricade.

Once you have them and wish to get rid of them, there are only a few options.

First, the repeated mowing or cutting of emerging shoots or stolons at ground level before they reach any size will usually kill the plants, but it often takes more than one growing season.

Second, you can try to dig them up, a process that works for the smaller species but gets to be very expensive when dealing with the larger types.

Third, bamboo culms can be killed with applications of a glyphosate herbicide, but again, it often takes time. You must cut each culm off at ground level, brush with the herbicide, then repeat the process often throughout the growing season.

10

Weedy Annuals and Biennials

The following plants are weeds of lawn and garden and except for a few behemoths such as giant hogweed or Mexican bamboo, most are easily recognized as being smaller than a shrub. If they die at year's end and only come back from seed, they are annuals. If they germinate in one year but wait for the second year to bloom and fruit, they are biennials. If they come back from the roots, year after year, they are perennials.

Annual Weeds

Many annual and biennial weeds fall into the ruderal classification, because they have a short life span in which to pack what other plants take years to achieve. Ruderals are noted for their high seed output. They are also known poetically as "seeds of the troubled earth." That is, they often germinate in disturbed soil, soil that has been tossed and turned about by highway departments, road builders, or developers (also, by home gardeners who begin to garden in earth that is comparatively new).

Some of these weeds can germinate, flower, and seed within a span of weeks. The following are all star-class ruderals.

Ragweed

Every autumn, year after year, goldenrod (*Solidago* spp.) gets bad press about hay fever, while the real culprit, ragweed (*Ambrosia* spp.), is ignored. Ragweed is the number one cause of autumn hay fever because at that time of year the plants release clouds of pollen (a single plant can produce up to one billion pollen grains) and the wind carries the pollen for tens of miles. The pollen of goldenrod (which unfortunately flowers about the same time) is far too heavy to be airborne.

There are two kinds of annual ragweed that cause most of the allergy problems: Short ragweed (*Ambrosia artemisifolia*) and giant ragweed (*A. trifida*). They both grow in abandoned or recently disturbed land and plants are found throughout the country.

Short ragweed grows up to five feet tall and bear highly cut leaves (usually alternate but sometimes opposite) and drooping, inconspicuous green flowers on erect spikes, which bloom in late summer and early fall. Giant ragweed can reach heights of fifteen feet, and its stems and leaves have stiff hairs that are rough to the touch. The opposite leaves are deeply three-lobed, with pointed tips. Flowers are similar to the above.

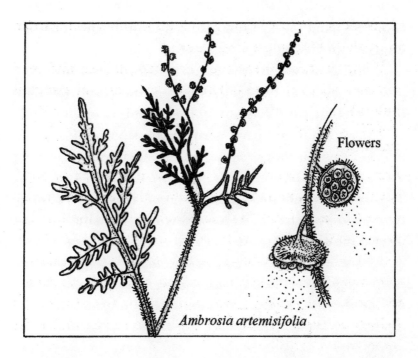

Flowers

Ambrosia artemisifolia

Method of Removal: *Because ragweed thrives in disturbed ground, the best prevention is to keep open but unused land planted with annual or perennial grasses or forage plants. Small populations can be controlled by pulling up the plants, but always do the job before flowering begins. Glyphosate herbicides will work.*

Cornflowers

Cornflowers (*Centaurea cyanus*), also called bachelor buttons or bluebottles, are annuals that sport brilliant deep blue flowers and have long been favorites in English cottage gardens or flower collections for cutting gardens. The common name of cornflowers refers to their presence in English cornfields.

Cornflowers are hardy annuals, with narrow and cottony silver leaves, and long stems up to two feet tall that bear rich blue, thistlelike blooms (sometimes in pink, red, or white), blooming from early to late summer on. They tolerate dry soil, hot weather, and are generally not fussy about their surroundings.

More of a nuisance than a threat, cornflowers weed freely and eventually take over territory, choking out native wildflowers and grasses.

Method of Removal: *Hand-pull seedlings, trying to remove plants before they set seed. If that fails, a glyphosate herbicide can be carefully used.*

The Sacred Datura

At one time I would grow one plant of the jimson weed or the sacred datura (*Datura stramonium*) at our front stoop. Most of the foliage was hidden behind the luxurious leaves of white four-o'clocks (*Mirabilis jalapa*), a vesper plant grown by Thomas Jefferson in his Monticello garden.

A few years ago, the United Parcel Service man brushed against a few of the leaves that grew out and over the other plants while he happened to be wearing the obligatory summer uniform of brown shorts. A few days later, I noticed a rash on his leg exactly at the right height for this beautiful weed to brush his skin.

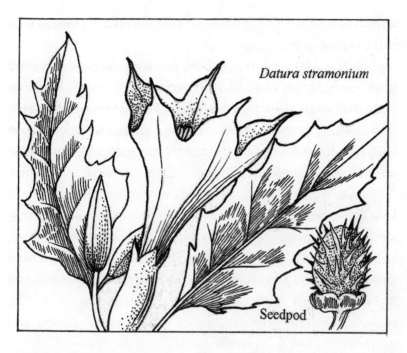

Datura stramonium

Seedpod

"It's contact dermatitis," he said. "I must have brushed up against something that I'm allergic to."

"Poison ivy?"

"Could be but I've never been bothered before."

I volunteered no other information but made sure that I moved the one specimen of jimson weed a bit farther to the left.

Once recognized, datura (*Datura stramonium*) is high on anyone's list of troublesome weeds. Like many natural threats, the plant has a number of common names including jimson weed (a corruption of Jamestown weed), the devil's trumpet, angel's trumpet, the apple of Peru, mad apple, Feng Ch'Ieh Erh, Estramonio, Doornappelkruid, or the Concombre Zombie.

Daturas are annuals that bear large unpleasant-smelling alternate leaves, the edges irregularly wavy-toothed. In good soil they often reach a height of five feet but usually stay around three. Leaves are often pockmarked because they are viewed as exceptional treats by flea beetles. The late-afternoon- and evening-blooming flowers are exquisite and produce a sweet scent upon opening.

The seedpods are very strange looking, resembling something found in a Salvador Dali painting. Pigeon egg–sized and shaped fruits are covered with thorns and densely packed with seeds. They are pantropic weeds and are also found throughout the temperate zones of the world. They are often found in fields, waste places, and generally weedy surroundings.

The name of *Datura* is said to have been coined by Linnaeus from *dare*, "to give," because the plants were given to those whose sexual powers had weakened. *Webster's Second International Dictionary* lists a different source: the Hindu word, *dhatura*, which simply means "the plant." This time I'll side with the dictionary.

Neltje Blanchan said that the Indians called datura the white man's plant, and also associated it with the Jamestown settlement. She asserts that Raleigh's colonists would have been more than likely to carry with them the seeds of this herb because it yielded an alkaloid more esteemed in the England of their day, than the alkaloid of opium known as morphine. Datura was smoked by asthmatics (DANGER!) and gardeners of that time were said to only banish it from their yards because of the "rank odor of the leaves."

It was used by many Native American tribes in religious ceremonies to induce hallucinations. In fact, there are connections between these hallucinations and the amazing visions of the Oracle at Delphi back in Ancient Greece.

Gardeners and anybody with a backyard should be advised that present day references to the chemical uses of medicinal plants point out the whole plant contains atropine and other alkaloids. Atropine is used in the treatment of eye diseases to dilate pupils and, because it impedes the action of the parasympathetic nervous system, has been a treatment for Parkinson's disease. The plant has also been used to make behind-the-ear patches that combat vertigo. But many fatalities have been recorded over the years and people with sensitive skin must be careful of contact dermatitis. Never put fingers that have touched the leaves anywhere near the eye.

Method of Removal: Because daturas are annuals, they are easier to control than many of the weeds in this book. Never let a plant go to seed. Mow or cut plants off at ground level.

Hairy Galinsoga

A number of weeds arrived on American shores through the interventions of botanical gardens. One such weed is hairy galinsoga (*Galinsoga ciliata*), thought to have first appeared on the scene sometime in the mid-1830s at Bartram's Garden in Philadelphia.

These cosmopolitan weeds have opposite, oval to triangular, coarsely toothed leaves, densely covered with hairs on the top but with the hairs limited to the veins on the leaf bottom. They reach a height of about two feet. Flowers are small and look like little daisies that have lost most of their petals. Five, sometimes four, white (rarely pink), three-notched petals (really ray flowers) surround the yellow disk.

In a perfect garden, these weeds would have their fibrous roots yanked out. Compared to some weeds, they are less than threatening. But, these plants can produce seed that often begins to germinate as soon as it hits the ground, so forewarned is forearmed. Because the seeds are referred to as "seeds of the troubled earth," they do not usually germinate in established ecosystems but thrive vigorously where the earth has been disturbed, especially where roads are being built or malls installed.

Method of Removal: *Pull them up when the earth is damp, making sure you do the job before they flower and set seed.*

Buffalobur

Another dastardly member of the tomato family is the buffalobur (*Solanum rostratum*). The name "buffalobur" goes back to the first settlers of the Great Plains, where the plant was abundant and distribution rested on buffalo carrying the burs on their shaggy coats. It's a native of the American Midwest and has recently been seen spreading across the country. Look for this weed on disturbed land, waste areas, abandoned farms, and barnyards. The burs are known to damage sheep's wool.

Buffalobur is a low growing, yellow-flowered, spined, hairy annual. The stems are erect and bushy, up to two feet long. Except for the flowers, the entire plant is adorned with sharp spines, which are dangerous, and if you inadvertently step on one of the bristly fruits, you'll know it. Alternate leaves from two to six inches long are cut into five to seven lobes (sometimes again into smaller lobes) and they are covered with prickles. The flowers are five-lobed, wheel-shaped, from an inch to an inch and a half across, blooming in spined clusters. The prickly calyx matures into a spiny bur that covers the seedpod.

Method of Removal: You must pull up young plants before they go to seed. Mow the plants just above ground level or hoe them up, again, before seeds form. Little is known about using a safe herbicide so, if infestations are large and beyond hand control, contact your local extension agent.

Chickweed

Common chickweed (*Stellaria media*), or stichwort, is an annual weed that in warmer climes, will flower on and off throughout the year.

Branching, prostrate stems bear opposite simple leaves and sport a line of hairs that run along the stalk until meeting a pair of leaves, and then switch sides until meeting the next pair of leaves. Little five-petalled flowers resemble white stars (hence the genus name, *Stellaria,* from the Latin for star), bloom in late winter or early spring, soon maturing into fruit capsules that hold many seeds. One mature chickweed can produce about 15,000 seeds. An invasion of chickweed can cover the ground for many feet and it is an awesome task to be rid of it.

Method of Removal: Chickweed is a weed of poor soil and disturbed earth. Remove the plants by pulling them up, but do the job before they go to seed.

Biennial Weeds

Biennial weeds are those that take two seasons to complete a life cycle. The first year, they usually begin life as leafy rosettes that hug the ground. The second year, the plant goes into vertical growth, produces flowers, seeds, and then passes from the scene. Sometimes, dependent on climate and physical conditions, some biennials become short-term perennials, but they never last very long.

Wild Burdocks

One of the clues to a society's acceptance or rejection of a plant can be measured by the number of common

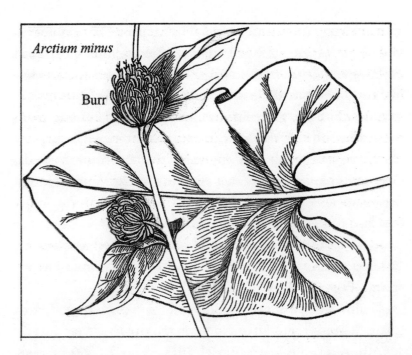

names. Often, the more names, the more rejection it has received. Burdocks are despised weeds answering to the following: bardana, bardane, burdock root, beggar's buttons, burrburr, burrseed, clothburr, cocklebur, fox's clote, stick-buttons, and turkey burr. Burdocks belong to genus *Arctium*, derived from the Greek word *arktos*, meaning bear. Natives of Eurasia, they are now widely established in North America

Common or lesser burdock (*Arctium minus*) is considered a medicinal plant, but that's the only thing in its favor. In recent years, this plant has gained its foothold on more and more territory, actually becoming commonplace where once it was rare. The reason? The spread of the species is directly linked to the marvelous mechanics of its seed, for here is the inspiration of our commercial Velcro®. The burlike fruit readily clings to animal fur and human clothing. For that reason, farmers take these weeds as serious threats to sheep because the burs damage the quality of the wool. In some areas, common burdock has become so abundant that it's currently a dominant understory species.

Usually described as biennials, common burdock can grow for a number of seasons before flowering, thus becoming a short-lived perennial where circumstances demand. But once it blooms, the plant dies.

Common burdock produces a basal rosette of large ovate leaves, rising from a taproot up to three feet in length. Alternate leaves march up four to six feet of stem, blooming on top with globular flower-heads containing purple thistlelike flowers surrounded by hook-tipped bracts. When ripe, the spiny burs of the fruit readily attach to cloth.

The closely related species, great burdock (*A. lappa*), also came to North America from Europe but is not as common as *A. minus*.

Great burdock is also a biennial (or short-lived perennial) that is grown around the world for its medicinal and herbal properties. It's also a popular vegetable in Japan where it's known as *gobo*.

Method of Removal: Pull up plants when young. Older plants can be cut off at ground level, then treated with applications of a glyphosate herbicide but always follow these steps before plants bloom and seed.

Garlic Mustard

Like most pest plants, garlic mustard (*Alliaria petiolata*) goes by many common names, including hedge garlic, sauce-alone, Jack-by-the-hedge, poor man's mustard, and garlic-wort (*wort* being a Middle English word for plant).

The plant arrived on our shores back in the late 1860s and was first reported on Long Island, New York. Since then, it's gone north, south, and west with a vengeance. Once established, it spreads and takes over by preventing the growth of native plants and wildflowers.

Garlic mustard is a biennial herb with seedlings emerging in late winter to early spring, forming basal rosettes by midsummer. During the spring of the following year, the rosettes generate floral stalks, followed by blossoming and setting seed.

Kidney-shaped basal leaves are dark green, and have scalloped edges. The stem leaves are alternate, sharply toothed, and triangular in shape. When crushed there is a distinct garlic odor.

During the second year, the rosettes send up one to many single floral stalks that bear white, mustardlike flowers with four petals. The fruits ripen in early summer. Each fruit can contain up to sixteen seeds, so a single plant is capable of producing some 8,000 seeds. The seeds lie dormant for up to a year before germination the following spring.

These plants are guilty of displacing native plants, and are fond of invading all sorts of soil, especially along the edges of woodlands, where they find partial shade.

Method of Removal: Watch for plants and remove them as soon as you spot them, before they go to seed. Plants can be pulled up by hand but it works best early in the season when roots are not strong and the ground is moist. You can also mow the plants but you must keep it up. Applications of glyphosate work quite well with larger populations.

Musk Thistle

Nodding or musk thistles (*Carduus nutans*) have been considered noxious weeds ever since their introduction from Eurasia, back in the mid-1800s. This weed ranks number three on the "Most Wanted List" of the so-called "bad seeds," with twenty-two states banning it.

Musk thistles are opportunists and, as such, classified as annuals, winter annuals, or biennials. Usually the seeds produced in the summer of one year germinate, overwinter as a rosette of leaves, then blossom and seed the following spring. They are at home in abandoned fields, pastures, and waste places in general, from Canada south to the Carolinas and west to Missouri.

The lance-shaped leaves are up to ten inches long, deeply lobed, and very spiny, their bases extending up and down the stems like prickly wings. Nodding, thistlelike, usually over two inch wide flowers of rose-purple bloom on top of long stalks, the stalks often covered with hairs resembling a cobweb. The fruits are barbed bristles.

Each fruit produces a host of seeds, with a plant total of some 10,000 seeds per season. The wind buffets their accompanying thistledown, allowing the seeds to travel many miles. Again, these are seeds of the troubled earth, finding a home in disturbed and bare soil.

Method of Removal: *Using gloves, remove individual plants before they go to seed.*

Poison Hemlock

Meet poison hemlock (*Conium maculatum*), a highly toxic plant that was used to poison Socrates, a plant that has no relationship to the large genus of conifers known as hemlocks, belonging to the genus *Tsuga*.

This is one tough plant and every part of it is toxic! Even touching this plant can result in contact dermatitis. Children have been stricken because they have tried to use the hollow stems as straws of peashooters. Avoid handling without gloves.

A biennial (or short-lived perennial), poison hemlock grows throughout the world, and was brought to the United States as a traditional folk cancer remedy that did not work. Today it continues to spread, especially north to Canada and south to the Carolinas.

Purple-spotted, hollow stems branch in many directions, reaching a height of about six feet. The leaves are carrotlike, with many divisions, and ill-scented when crushed or bruised. The small, white flowers bloom in small umbels, bunched together to make a larger disk and look a great deal like Queen Anne's lace. But the umbels have more distance between them than does Queen Anne's lace and lack its small purple flower in the center. Plants reproduce only from seed, with some seeds germinating in the fall, producing flowers the following spring. The seeds easily cling to the fur of animals or to human clothing and are easily distributed.

Plants are common along roadsides and the edges of fields, especially in areas with moist soil or standing water.

Method of Removal: Hand-pulling is best but remember to wear gloves and dispose of the plants in a careful manner. It is not necessary to pull up all the roots since the few that are left rarely produce new plants. Remember to do the work before the plants flower.

Queen Anne's Lace

A lovely wildflower to some and a weed to others, Queen Anne's lace (*Daucus Carota* var. *carota*) is the wild plant that led to the development of the common carrot. The weeds of today probably came from colonial gardens when carrot seeds escaped and reverted to the original wild plant.

This wild carrot is a biennial that in its second year forms a taproot that resembles a sad carrot. It also shares the distinctive smell of the vegetable. The height can reach two feet, with stems sporting very finely divided leaves, much like a feather. Stems and leaves are covered with fine hairs. The umbels of small white flowers form a flat disk some three or four inches wide. After flowers are fertilized, the disk folds up and looks like a small brown basket or fanciful bird's nest. The central flower of each disk is purple or dark red.

Susceptible people can develop skin irritations from exposure to the sap when in the sunlight.

Method of Removal: *Before flowering, hand-pull the plants or mow large infestations close to the ground.*

Common Foxglove

The common foxglove (*Digitalis purpurea*) is a beautiful and time-honored garden plant, important to gardeners and to medicine. Born in 1741, William Withering of Shropshire, England, was the first doctor credited with linking the cardiac glycosides found in the plant to their actions on the human heart. Because of these potentially poisonous properties, plants are completely no-maintenance, and shunned by the deer population.

Foxgloves are usually biennials (rarely short-lived perennials), having dark green or white-woolly leaves, almost a foot long, usually found growing in a basal rosette. During the first year the plants develop root systems and during the second year they produce the flowers stalks that can reach a height of five feet. Up to two inches long, tubular or bell-shaped, drooping flowers appear in shades of purple, lavender, pink, cream, or white, often dappled with colored spots. They bloom in late spring and early summer.

Thought to have originally come from the western Mediterranean region, they have been naturalized for centuries in much of Europe and in England, and were probably brought to this country by early settlers.

Foxgloves seed with such proficiency that they become weeds in many gardens. If their story ended there, they would not be such a problem. But they are extremely poisonous to both animals and humans, killing countless farm animals every year and also taking their toll on people who either use the leaves improperly as a heart restorative or mistake the leaves for another herb called comfrey.

Digitalis lantana, the Grecian foxglove, has escaped in various parts of the Midwest, including large infestations in Kansas. Again, plants are poisonous to both animals and humans, and because there are such high concentrations of digitalis in the leaves of the Grecian variety, it is important that you wear gloves when handling this plant.

Method of Removal: *The plants are easy to pull up by hand the first year, but you must be vigilant because the seeds continue to produce new plants for at least another year. To date, herbicides have little effect.*

Teasels

The common and cut-leaved teasel (*Dipsacus sylvestris*) came to North America in the 1700s, brought over by owners of textile mills. The stiff seedpods were used to remove impurities from wool and to raise the nap on felt. As a result, the plants are still found in the vicinities of long-abandoned mills and warehouses. The common name of teasel comes from "teasing" material.

Teasels are biennials or monocarpic short-lived perennials. Seedlings begin as basal rosettes, remaining in that state of development for a year or they overwinter. Plants may grow to a height of six feet. The stems are marked with ridges and rows of down-pointing spines. Veins and midribs have spines. Leaves often have fused bases that collect water. As they age, the plants develop long taproots. Small, purple flowers are produced in dense floral heads, each protected by spinelike bracts. Teasels bloom from midsummer on.

Plants are found along roadsides, wasteland, abandoned farms, and continue to spread along the interstate highway systems, in part because of the number of seeds they produce and the seed heads being picked up and moved by road machinery. They are also popular in dried flower arrangements and when these bouquets are tossed away, the seeds within the decorative dried seed heads are still viable. The plants compete with pasture grasses and wildflowers, and can choke out many desirable species.

Method of Removal: Remove plants before they seed using any of the weeders used for tap-rooted plants. Or cut the blooms off at the base of the rosette but only after flowers have formed and opened. Usually the roots will not rebloom. Glyphosate may also be used during the dormant season.

Honesty

Honesty, or as it's sometimes called, the money plant (*Lunaria annua*) is a biennial plant traditionally found in cutting gardens where its dried, silver seedpods have long been valued in dried bouquets.

Honesty is a native of southeastern Europe and western Asia, and has now naturalized in many parts of the United States. Plants escaped from gardens as the wind blew the dried, flat seedpods (called siliculas) or when seeds wound up in landfills after dusty and worn winter bouquets were tossed out.

Plants grow two to three feet high and have stiff and hairy stems that bear coarse, simple, broad, toothed leaves. Usually by the second year of growth, they bloom with three-foot stalks of many purple or white four-petalled flowers. These plants are often used as floral bedding plants in European gardens, and tossed out before seedpods form.

Method of Removal: *Pull up plants by hand before they flower or go to seed.*

White and Yellow Sweet Clover

White sweet clover (*Melilotus alba*) and yellow sweet clover (*M. officinalis*) thrive in lawns, open fields, meadows, and abandoned lands throughout the country. Both plants and seed were brought over to America by the settlers, along with the honeybee. You can see the plants growing along backcountry roads where the tall spikes of the white clover wave in the wind stream of your car.

Both these clovers have stout taproots, are drought tolerant, and quite hardy. White sweet clover is a bit more tolerant of standing water than is yellow sweet clover. These plants are good indicators of sweet or sour soil and they grow best in calcareous soils with pH levels of 6.5 or higher.

White sweet clover has pinnately divided leaves with three lanceolate-shaped, toothed leaflets, and reaches a height from one to ten feet. White pealike flowers bloom in spikelike racemes, with thirty to eighty flowers on each spike. When crushed, the leaves have the fragrance of new-mown hay.

Yellow sweet clover is much the same except plants only reach heights of two feet and the pealike flowers are yellow blooming on four-inch-long racemes. When crushed, the leaves smell of vanilla because they contain coumarin, a chemical used to flavor cheese.

Both species flower in June and July. Usually, the yellow precedes the white by a few weeks. Both are true biennials, flowering and dying in the second year.

Although a number of insects visit these flowers, the principle pollinator is the honeybee.

These clovers are also "seeds of the troubled earth" and their seeds retain viability for over twenty years or more. They remain dormant until conditions are just right for germination.

If kept in enclosed areas these plants would be controllable but once out in the world they become invasive exotics and a threat to the existing populations of native plants and wild flowers.

Method of Removal: *Hand-pull seedlings in the first year or mow them as close to the earth as possible.*

Common Mullein or Woolly Mullein

The common mullein (*Verbascum thapsus*) or as it's sometimes called, the woolly mullein, is a fascinating plant with a long horticultural history. This was the plant that was a high point in Roman funerals when the tall, dried stalks were soaked in oil, and then lit for a hero's entrance into another world.

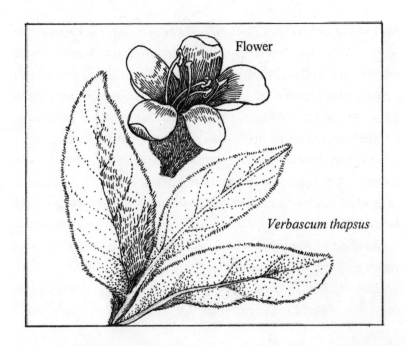

Flower

Verbascum thapsus

Originally found in both Europe and Asia, the plants were brought over to America by settlers as a medicinal herb, used especially for treating asthma, coughs, and in making earache drops. It was also used as a narcotic fish poison. But remember, it's considered somewhat dangerous and many people are susceptible to contact dermatitis from the many hairs on the leaves and stems.

Common mulleins are biennials. The first year mullein plants are low-growing rosettes of attractive, gray-green, felty leaves up to a foot long. They winter over and the following spring will send up flowering stalks often ten feet high. Yellow, five-petalled flowers bloom up and down the stem but only a few at a time. The tiny seeds travel easily and have a long soil life, capable of germination even after fifty or more years. A single plant can produce upwards of 150,000 seeds.

Mulleins are a threat because once established, they easily crowd out more desirable native plants and even shrubs. Plants are at home along back roads, open meadows, abandoned fields, wastelands, and the edges of woodlands.

Method of Removal: *Young plants are easily recognized and easily pulled up from the dry soil they prefer. Never let them go to seed. A glyphosate herbicide can also be used where the lay of the land makes hand-pulling impractical.*

11

Perennial Weeds
and Mosses

Most perennial weeds belong in a class of plants called competitors. These weeds are usually bigger than their garden neighbors and, like the thugs on the street, muscle in through girth and strength alone. They succeed by dint of this muscle and often tower over their competition or have invasive root systems that move so quickly they can inspire thoughts of the Indy 500.

Goutweed

I can't believe it! Nurseries still sell this pernicious weed, describing it as a great groundcover. Also known as bishop's weed, herb Gerard, ash-weed, and in England as ground elder, *Aegopodium podagraria* is the kind of plant that sends hackles up whenever gardeners congregate and talk about falling for the siren song of nursery advertising. English gardeners are adamant about this being one of the worst weeds ever, and are appalled that Americans still

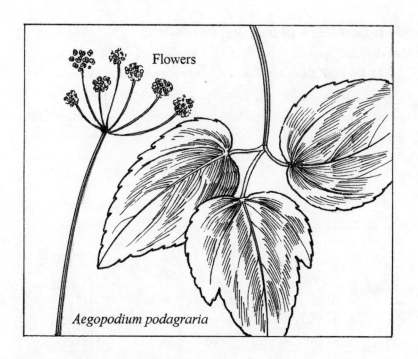

Flowers

Aegopodium podagraria

plant the variegated form (*A. podagraria 'Variegatum'*) because it lacks some chlorophyll that supposedly weakens
the plant so it's less of a pest. Don't you believe it.

This perennial groundcover grows about a foot high,
and consists of basal crowns all connected by rampaging
rhizomes. The leaves are usually three leaflets with ser-
rated edges, joined in a compound leaf. Color is a pale
gray-green with splotches of white or a cream color varie-
gation. The leaves can easily scorch under hot sun. Flowers
appear on slightly taller stalks, are flat discs of small white
flowers similar to those found on Queen Anne's lace. Lit-

tle brown seeds appear on the fruiting stalks and should be deadheaded to prevent self-sowing.

Method of Removal: Broken rhizomes root with ease so don't dig up plants unless you get them all. Repeated mowings will do the job but you must persist all summer. Or use a glyphosate herbicide, early in the year.

Creeping Bugleweed

Creeping bugleweed (*Ajuga reptans*) is an attractive groundcover that is sold by many nurseries and is represented by a number of colorful cultivars. But if you love your lawn, any invader, no matter how charming, should be viewed as an enemy and bugleweed is just that. Over a short period of time, the plants spread by interlocking runners and soon form mats of foliage that are so dense that not only weeds have trouble growing, but grasses, too. Soon after introduction, bugleweed will leave the original boundaries and enter the lawn.

In addition, the variegated forms often revert to their humbler origins and produce additional chlorophyll (thanks to losing the variegations), becoming even stronger invaders.

Bugleweeds are semi-evergreen groundcovers, between two and four inches tall, but when flowering are up to ten inches in height. Leaves are light green to dark green, oven-bronzed, purple, or have striped variegations. The flowers are small, blue, purple, or white, and look like tiny snapdragons.

Method of Removal: *The best way to remove bugleweed is to dig up individual plants using a fishtail or a gooseneck weeder. Infestations are usually too small to justify the use of chemical controls.*

Wild Garlic

Wild garlic (*Allium vineale*) is often confused with wild onion (*A. canadense*) but the two are easily distinguished by looking at the leaves: If the leaves are flat, the plant is wild onion but if the leaves are round and hollow, it's wild garlic. Both plants smell strongly of garlic.

Wild garlic, also known as field garlic, crow's garlic, and stag garlic, is a serious weed in both the northeastern and southeastern United States. Not only is it a pest to dairy farmers (because once cattle begin to graze on the plant, their milk is tainted), but to home gardeners and lawn lovers, too.

The plants spring up from bulbs. The bunches of hollow leaves usually stay under a foot high. Plants rarely flower but instead produce a cluster of little bulbils on top of an erect stem. If they do bloom, the flowers are small, open in a cluster, and have pale rose to greenish to white petals. Seeds are quite rare. Sometimes the bulbils actually start to grow while still attached to the parent plant.

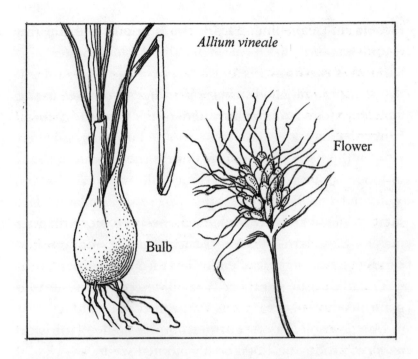

Method of Removal: *Pulling up the plants by hand or using a tool to extract weeds is best but you must remove the entire bulb. It's best to do this early in the year before the bulbils form.*

Canada Thistle

The Canada thistle (*Cirsium arvense*) is a noxious perennial weed, with prickly leaves and a tenaciously creeping rootstock. The plants were introduced from Eurasia into North America back in the early 1600s and have been threatening native plants ever since. It's found north from Maine to California, up into Canada, and south to below the Mason-Dixon line. This plant is one of the top five "Most Wanted" weed pests in the United States and banned by twenty-nine states.

Erect and branched stems reach a height of three to five feet, are ridged like celery, and often have short hairs. Lance-shaped leaves have spiny, toothed margins and alternate on the stems. Rose-purple flowers (rarely white), begin to bloom in early summer, arranged in rounded clusters. Male and female flowers appear on separate plants. The small single-seed fruits (called achenes) are more than an inch long and have a feathery structure at the seed base that clings to fabric and fur or easily flies through the air.

Canada thistle is especially troublesome because each plant produces lateral roots that can reach eighteen feet in one growing season. Furthermore, a single plant is capable of producing 1,500 bristly-plumed seeds.

Plants grow on abandoned farms, wasteland, old fields and pastures, and in old landfills. When they invade grasslands, they shade out and eventually destroy a host of native plants. As are walnuts, they are believed capable of releasing chemicals that inhibit the growth of competing plants.

Method of Removal: *Cut back mature plants before they flower and go to seed. Then treat with a glyphosate herbicide. The seeds have a long soil life, so vigilance is necessary.*

Crown Vetch

I've watched the spread of crown vetch (*Coronilla varia*) along the highways and byways of the Northeast and

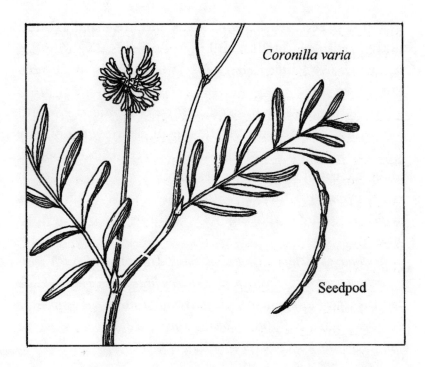

Coronilla varia

Seedpod

Southeast as highway department after highway department planted this pest in order to control erosion and cut back on maintenance. Originally from Europe and northern Africa, the plants were introduced into America back in the 1950s.

Vetch is a low-growing perennial member of the pea family, with dark green pairs of leaflets, some five to twelve pairs on a stem, and pale pink to lavender (rarely white) pealike blossoms that bloom most of the summer. Creeping stems can reach a length of six feet. Fruiting consists of narrow, leathery seedpods up to three inches long.

Plants prefer open, sunlit areas and are usually found along roadsides, ditches, and in open fields. I've found it as an invasive while walking backwoods trails in western North Carolina.

Spreading rapidly by seed and by creeping stems and roots, most native plants in the way of crown vetch quietly die. Instead of an area rich with a variety of native plants, you get acres of solitary crown vetch.

Yet even with the knowledge that this is a dangerous weed, highway departments continue to buy it and plant it.

Method of Removal: *Control small plantings of vetch with continued mowing. You can also cover plants with black plastic and bake them in the summer sun. A treatment with a glyphosate herbicide in the fall and following spring will eliminate plants that regenerate from roots or sprout from seed.*

The Wild Artichoke or Cardoon

Cardoons (*Cynara cardunculus*) are great garden plants, known for providing stunning backgrounds of statuesque gray-green foliage. The plants are also the original parents of that popular vegetable, the artichoke; and cardoons were also cultivated for their edible roots and their thickened leafstalks, ingredients very popular in Italian cooking. But since their introduction in the 1860s, to both the east and the west coast, plants have spread and become threatening weeds.

Deeply cut leaves are gray-green above and have whitish short wooly hairs beneath, often up to three feet long, and rise from a bushy rosette to a height of six feet with a plant diameter of five inches. Flower stalks are two to three inches in diameter, with the big, purplish blue thistlelike flowers opening from spiny receptacles. In the globe artichoke (*Cynara scolymus*), the bases of the fleshy receptacle are edible. There is a sizable taproot.

When he traveled there in 1832, Charles Darwin described these plants as covering the Argentine wilderness. "The whole country," he wrote, "may be called one great bed of these plants."

Today, they have invaded parts of California where they can number up to 22,000 plants per acre. Once established, they easily drive out all the native plants where they form monocultures of their own. The only thing to say in their favor is the popularity of their seeds with some birds—leading, of course, to the eventual spread of *more* cardoons.

Method of Removal: When you spot the young seedlings, pull the long, perennial taproot. You can cut the plants off at the base, then treat the stump with a glyphosate herbicide.

Field Bindweed

Often called wild morning glory, the field bindweed *Convolvulus arvensis* is known throughout the world of farming as a terrible weed. It was probably introduced to America in the mid 1700s and spread west thanks to the development of the railroads. This horror-plant is ranked number five on the "Most Wanted" list of weeds in the United States, with seventeen states banning it. It is among the ten worst weeds in the world.

Some of the more descriptive common names are: possession vine, creeping Jenny, and creeping Charlie. Like Charlie and Jenny, field bindweed is a creeping and vining perennial, originally from Europe, that twists along the ground and climbs counterclockwise around almost any support. Its roots can extend fifteen or more feet, penetrating deep within the soil.

Leaves are arrow-shaped and up to four inches long. The funnel-like flowers have five fused petals, usually white to a pale pink. The vines can grow up to ten feet long. Seed capsules usually contain up to ten seeds. The seeds can remain viable for over fifty years.

Although usually only a threat to commercial farmers, the bindweeds have, thanks to interstate travel, spread all over the country and are often unwanted invaders into the home garden. Their deep roots take nutrition and water from the soil, and if left unchecked, can wind around tall perennials and bring them crashing (usually silently), down. Bindweeds are now a serious problem throughout the country, except in the hotter parts of the Southeast.

Method of Removal: *Hand-pull the plants as soon as spotted, preferably when the soil is moist. You will have to do it more than once. Carefully applied applications of a glyphosate herbicide will* usually work. For large infestations, it's best to contact your extension agent.

Barren Strawberry

At home in the Far East, the barren strawberry (*Duchesnea indica*) traveled from there to India and then entered the United States sometime in the eighteenth century.

It grows as a semi-evergreen trailing perennial with rather plain yellow five-petalled flowers, each rising from the axil of a three-parted leaf. About four to five inches high, it's often found creeping along in waste places, preferring the shade. The fruits appear in late summer, resembling small strawberries but are dry and tasteless.

Method of Removal: I must confess when I found it in my garden, I let it be. But if the plants get out of hand, use a good weeder and make sure you get the entire crown. If it persists, it might be a good idea to look for a more attractive groundcover.

Leafy Spurge

The spurges are easy to identify because they have milky sap. The weed in question is the leafy spurge, or as it's often called, wolf's milk spurge (*Euphorbia esula*). Here's a plant that has invaded much of the United States and continues to conquer new territory every year. This spurge was discovered in the early 1800s when it arrived in Massachusetts as a seed impurity imported from Europe and

Asia. As of today, it ranks number four on the "Most Wanted" list of weeds in the United States, with nineteen states banning it.

This spring they were blooming in my garden, the seeds traveling from a vacant lot down the street. Plants are erect, branching perennials, between two and three feet tall, with small oval to pale green, lance-shaped leaves. Clustered stems grow from a vertical root that extends for many feet.

This plant belongs to the same genus as the popular Christmas plant, the poinsettia (*Euphorbia pulcherrima*), but instead of having large red petal-like bracts (really modified leaves), it has smaller bright yellow bracts. In both cases, the flowers are very small and easily overlooked. The yellow bracts open from April to June, depending on your latitude, and the greenish yellow flowers appearing later.

Leafy spurge seeds have extended viability and remain active for at least seven years. And as with many plants, the seed capsules open with a snap so seeds fly in all directions—up to fifteen feet or more from the parent. In addition to the seeds, wandering roots give rise to new plants.

I've seen leafy spurge do its thing as it displaces some of the native vegetation in that aforementioned vacant lot. Among the plants that have disappeared are blue-eyed grass (*Iris* spp.), strawberries (*Fragaria virginiana*), and the star chickweed (*Stellaria pubera*).

If that weren't enough, like black walnuts, the plants produce toxins that inhibit the growth of any competitors. Add their thirst for water and nutrients to their above-listed faults, and you have a mean weed.

Method of Removal: The only good thing about getting rid of leafy spurge is that plants usually grow in thick patches, so repeated mowings will keep it at bay until the roots weaken and die. A single mowing will just stimulate new growth. Glyphosate herbicides can also be used. Again, because the plants grow in thick patches, the danger of killing innocents is reduced.

Ground Ivy or Gill-Over-the-Ground

Ground ivy (*Glechoma hederacea*) is found around the world, spread about by explorers and emigrants, tourists and travelers, as well as animals and birds. It's one of those weeds that sends up the hackles of most folks who love lawns—although as a groundcover, it's one of the best.

Ground ivy is a creeping, ivy-like perennial, with dark green, opposite, round to kidney-shaped leaves, somewhat downy and having scalloped edges. Trailing square stems move about, rooting at occasional nodes. Two-lipped violet flowers, arise in whorls of leaf axils, blooming from late spring to summer.

The plant came to America with the settlers, who brought its seeds because ground ivy has a long tradition as a folk remedy, especially for asthma, backaches, and bruises. Many books warn that it's reportedly toxic to horses.

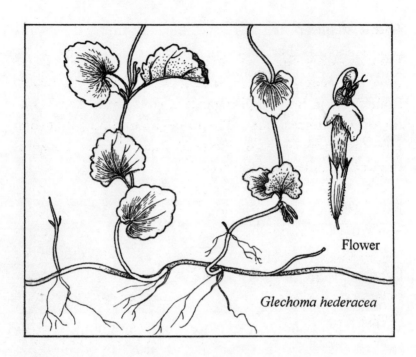

Flower

Glechoma hederacea

Because of its rooting proclivities, ground ivy can invade a lawn over a short period of time. Before reaching for the herbicide, it's often suggested that you study your lawn in a critical manner. Ground ivy, for example, does well in poor light, on poor soil, and likes a moist environment. It rarely makes headway in properly managed grasses.

Method of Removal: First try pulling up ground ivy on a cool morning after a rain. Usually the stems and roots come up in one long string. Use a glyphosate herbicide only if the act of weeding fails.

Giant Hogweed

I was growing the giant hogweed (*Herecleum manzagantium*) for years after first seeing it as a tower of beauty flourishing in fine English gardens (but I must admit, taking over Battersea Park). Then I began to notice that soon after the flowers had gone to seed, there were a number of hogweed seedlings in the area.

A member of the parsley/carrot family, hogweed, as its name implies, has a tendency to take over the garden. Sometimes in good soil and with fine weather, the plants can reach a height of twenty feet—in one summer. It was introduced into America as a garden subject, because once they had seen them in Europe, gardeners wanted them over here.

Today, hogweeds are found spreading on both the East and the West Coasts, the first wave coming from New York and the second wave beginning in Oregon and Washington. They prefer a site close to water or in damp soil.

The compound and deeply cut leaves of the giant hogweed can measure up to five feet across. Long stalks that resemble very large celery holds them. Flowers are small and white, but bloom in a very large, flat-topped umbel, with some umbels over two feet in diameter. Many fruits are produced that look like caraway seeds. The rootstock penetrates deep into the ground.

These plants are monocarpic perennials, which take several years (my first plant took five) to reach the blooming stage. The plant did persist for two more years before expiring because sometimes they produce additional crowns, which continue to flower and set seed.

When I had the plants in my garden, I had to warn people and children especially, not to touch the stems. That's because the stems have a clear, watery sap that contains toxins that are only active in the sunlight. These toxins cause photo-dermatitis in susceptible people. Touching the stem results in painful, burning blisters that can turn into purple scars. Children are at special risk because the stems are hollow and make great makeshift peashooters.

Method of Removal: *Care must be taken when touching hogweeds, so remember to wear gloves. Dig up any seedlings using a fishtail weeder. If confronted by a mature specimen, before it seeds, cut it off at ground level and brush the stump with a glyphosate herbicide.*

Lantana or Shrub Verbena

The shrub verbena (*Lantana camara*) is a tough beauty from the tropics, originally imported from the Caribbean and now naturalized in Florida and creeping northward.

Its oval leaves are rough, covered with fine hairs, and lie opposite on square hairy stems. The foliage has a distinct foxy odor that some people abhor. In a good season with plenty of heat, lantanas can reach a height of eight to ten feet, and are smothered in flowers all summer long. The individual flowers bloom in clusters, are tubular, with four petals, and come in a variety of colors from red to yellow to pink to white. Butterflies are partial to the flowers, which eventually produce glossy black fruits. These berries are poisonous to animals and humans, if taken in a large amount.

Plants have naturalized in Florida and are now moving into Georgia where they overwinter, looking dead on top but with live roots below.

It's not a problem north of USDA Zone 8 but once it goes wild in your southern garden, get rid of it.

Method of Removal: *Remove small plants by hand before they get large enough to flower and seed. A glyphosate herbicide is effective in small doses.*

Pepperweed

Pepperweed or tall whitetop (*Lepidium latifolium*) is also known as broadleaved pepperweed or ironweed, this last not to be confused with the beautiful wildflower, *Vernonia glauca*, known as ironweed, too.

These are highly invasive weeds that invade marshes and floodplains, and once established crowd out all the valuable native plants and wildflowers. Today it is known throughout the West and has recently been reported in coastal New England. They are natives of southeastern Europe and southwestern Asia.

Pepperweeds are perennials that form dense stands with stems up to five feet high. Beginning as a rosette of gray-green leaves, the eventual stems having alternate, lanceolate to elliptical leaves. The flowers bloom in panicles, with four green sepals and four white petals. Slightly flattened pods (known as silicles) produce reddish-brown seeds.

Method of Removal: *One suggestion to remove pepperweed is to flood the area where it grows. Hand-pulling before flowering is also recommended. A glyphosate herbicide can be effective but because these plants usually grow near water, care must be used in applications.*

Chinese Lespedeza

Chinese lespedeza (*Lespedeza cuneata*) originally came from eastern Asia. This perennial herb in the pea family was introduced into the Southeast as an erosion control plant and state agencies, pleased with the job the plant accomplished, sent it along to other states and other agencies. Now it's a major pest.

Chinese lespedeza can grow in a variety of habitats including severely eroded sterile soils. It will invade fields, abandoned pastures, open woodlands, prairies, borders of ponds and wetlands, fresh meadows, wastelands, and open disturbed ground. It must have full sun.

Plants range in height from three to five feet with alternate leaves, each divided into three smaller leaflets. The leaflets are covered with a dense layer of flat hairs, giving the plant a silvery appearance. Mature stems are fibrous and woody, with sharp, flat bristles. Flowers are violet to purple, blooming in clusters of two to four, arising from the axils of the upper leaves.

These weeds are a major threat because once they invade an area, they crowd out natives, then with spreading root systems, create a dense thicket that has no value to wildlife, including birds and insects.

Method of Removal: Because lespedeza has such a tough root system, it's impractical to pull up individual plants. Mowing is the best action, cutting the plants as close to the ground as possible. A dilute solution of a glyphosate herbicide is effective beginning in early summer.

Birdsfoot Trefoil

Imported as a pasture plant, birdsfoot trefoil (*Lotus corniculatus*) still has an enviable reputation with many farmers. An introduction from Europe, the seeds arrived in New York State in the 1880s where they were planted for erosion control and for forage.

Unlike the other members of the pea family, this trefoil has five leaflets instead of three, and either crawls along the ground or stands erect, varying between one and two feet high. The half-inch, pealike flowers are bright yellow, sometimes with little dots of red. They bloom in clusters of three to twelve individual blossoms. One-inch long brown seedpods resemble birds' feet.

Found throughout the United States and Canada, this trefoil escapes to be found in old fields, abandoned pastures, and often along the edges of country roads.

Like many invasive exotics, birdsfoot trefoil forms thick masses of intertwined stems that easily choke out more valuable native plants and wildflowers.

Method of Removal: *Repeated mowings of this plant close to the ground is an effective control.*

Gooseneck Loosestrife

This hardy perennial, accurately named the gooseneck loosestrife (*Lysimachia clethroides*), is described in nursery catalogs as "a vigorous-growing perennial." That means it spreads voraciously and takes over all in its path.

Plants grow in clumps, with reddish stems that bear lance-shaped, mid-green leaves that are yellow when young. Tiny, white, star-shaped flowers bloom in profusion on a stem. The tip of the stem nods when flowers are in bud but straightens out as they mature, rendering a perfect likeness of a goose neck. In their preferred soil, these plants often reach a three-foot height.

Plants spread by rhizomes that easily regenerate from any section left behind after digging.

Method of Removal: *Dig them up with care, or contain plantings behind barriers. They also lose some of their drive when planted in dry soil instead of the damp earth they really prefer.*

Purple Loosestrife

Purple loosestrife (*Lythrum salicaria*) ranks number two on the list of "Most Wanted" weed plants and is banned by

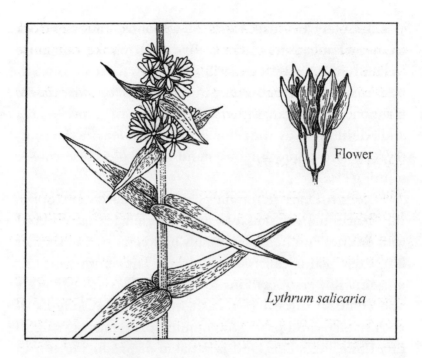

Flower

Lythrum salicaria

twenty-three states. This is a major, major pest and never, ever plant it, or even bother with the so-called sterile cultivars, in any garden under your control! You will still see plants for sale by nurseries that (let's hope) have no idea of what the plant is capable.

Like an invading horde, the original loosestrifes came to our shores in the early 1800s, brought here for ornamental and medicinal purposes. They thrive in Great Britain, most of Europe, parts of Russia, Japan, China, and northern India. According to the U.S. Fish and Wildlife Service, purple loosestrife is now found in every state except Florida.

Plants thrive in all kinds of wetlands, ranging from freshwater meadows to tidal marshes. If you've ever seen wetlands invaded by loosestrife, you know what an invasion by a noxious weed represents. In the years following its introduction, you can witness the demise of native plants and wildflowers as they bow to the invader. In the end, there is one homogeneous stand of purple loosestrife— nothing else.

Loosestrifes are perennials having a square stem, opposite, lance-shaped, stalkless, and whorled leaves, covered with down. Plant height is usually between two and six feet but a few plants can reach ten feet. The showy purplish magenta flowers sport four to six wrinkled petals. Flowers also come in three types, each with different lengths of both stamens and pistils. A blooming plant may have up to fifty flowering stems, and is capable of producing two to three million seeds every year. In addition, plants can spread vegetatively using underground stems that move about one foot per year.

Methods of Removal: *In small infestations pull up plants by hand, before seed ripens. For a larger siege, use a glyphosate herbicide, specifically designed for wetlands. If confronted by a truly large area full of these plants, contact your local extension agent or state agency.*

Pokeweed

For once we're writing about a good old American weed that, for a change, produced seeds purposely taken back to Europe instead of coming the other way. The plant's name is pokeweed (*Phytolacca americana*), a generally poisonous plant with spring shoots that early settlers found good to eat, (as long as they continually changed the cooking water). Civil War soldiers also used pokeberry ink for writing letters and American Indians used the plants' juice for staining leather and inscribing temporary tattoos. It should also be noted that great English gardens always contain at least one specimen of pokeweed—after all, just how often do you find a plant this large, which sports chartreuse flowers, red stems, and deep-purple berries?

Poke has a fascinating natural history: Its seeds were the favored food of America's now extinct bird, the passenger pigeon. Because these pigeons at one time existed in such numbers that they could cloud the sun when flying their migratory journeys, pokeweed is found almost everywhere in the country, except where the winters are really cold.

Pokeweeds can reach a height of ten feet, having succulent, purplish stems and large lance-shaped, shiny leaves with smooth, curled margins. Small, greenish flowers hang in drooping, grapelike clusters. Each flattened, spherical, green berry matures to a deep purple or almost-black fruit that contains ten seeds. Plants are usually found in old barnyards, open fields, abandoned land of all sorts, edges of roadsides, and gardens.

Method of Removal: *Pokeberry roots are deep so it's almost impossible to dig up plants once they are established. Pull seedlings up as soon as they appear. If you cut the plants off at soil level, be sure to apply a brushing of a glyphosate herbicide.*

Plantain

One of the common names for common plantain (*Plantago major*) is white-man's-foot, which points to its origin as a true exotic. It was probably introduced when it was intentionally brought over as a folk medicine or accidentally as seeds stuck to somebody's shoe. It now grows in most of the United States. The other common name is cart-track plant, again pointing a finger at the new arrivals on our shores.

The leaves are reputed to have anti-inflammatory and expectorant characteristics. The seeds are very high in mucilage and fiber, being closely related to the species *P. psyllium* and are a major ingredient in laxatives such as Metamucil®. The plants also provide food for wildlife including butterfly caterpillars. Some people may suffer from contact dermatitis after touching these weeds for any length of time.

Plantains are perennials, with large, thick, oval-shaped, wavy-margined or toothed, ribbed leaves and a heavy grooved stalk. The insignificant flowers bloom in a slender, elongated head on top of a tall stalk. They bloom from late spring into fall. *P. major atropurpurea* is a purple-leaved variety that is often grown in specialty rock gardens.

Plantains are generally weeds of the lawn, usually picking a sunny spot, often in the most visible place in your front yard.

Narrow-leaved plantain (*P. lanceolata*) bears lance-shaped leaves with three ribs. The tiny whitish flowers bloom in a short cylindrical head on a grooved stalk. They're usually found with the other species, in or near the lawn, in abandoned farmland, or vacant lots.

Method of Removal: *Hand-pick plantains using a good weeding tool, aiming for as much of the root as possible. Do this whenever you spot them in the lawn and never let the plants go to seed. You can also spot-treat them with a glyphosate herbicide. They can also be shaded out of existence.*

Japanese Knotweed

Commonly called Japanese knotweed, Mexican bamboo, or monkey bamboo, *Polygonum cuspidatum* is a vicious plant that is a member of the normally harmless buckwheat family (Polygonaceae). A native of eastern Asia, this species now invades both cultivated and waste areas throughout the northeastern United States and into southern Canada.

In 1825, the ever-busy nursery industry imported plants from Japan for English gardens and from there it journeyed to our shores in the late nineteenth century. In Japan, knotweeds grow in sunny places on hills, mountainsides, and volcanic slopes. In America, it grows just about anywhere it can find a place to sprout.

For a while, herbalists found value in using this knotweed as a laxative and a digestive enzyme but today we

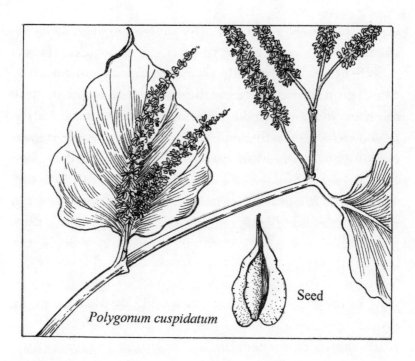

Polygonum cuspidatum   Seed

suspect that large amounts of condensed tannins may be carcinogenic.

This herbaceous perennial forms broad clumps or towering shoots, sometimes up to thirteen feet tall. They reproduce with seed or by their incredible rampaging rhizomes.

Stout stems are hollow and resemble bamboos (hence the common name of "Mexican bamboo"). Leaves, up to six inches long, are rounded or ovate, and come to a point. White flowers are small, bloom in clusters, and look like fleece. Plants spread by seed or stout rhizomes, which can travel almost twenty feet. The seeds are shiny blackish-brown and male and female flowers appear on different plants.

Polygonum cuspidatum is widely distributed in much of the eastern United States. In western Pennsylvania, it already occupies hundreds of acres of wetlands and is a particular problem along riverbanks, causing flooding by choking river and stream channels. Look for it in Colorado, Utah, northern California, Washington, Oregon, and Alaska, and on up into Canada. It has spread along the banks of the Allegheny and Ohio Rivers and I have personal memories of its domination of lots up in the Catskill Mountains of Sullivan County in upstate New York.

Once established, Japanese knotweed forms large, almost pure stands, which are very, very difficult to eradicate—almost immortal.

Method of Removal: *Digging up the entire plant can control small patches of this pest. But every tiny bit of rhizome must be removed, for like amoebas, each piece can regrow a new plant. Control larger infestations with persistent cutting but you must continue throughout the growing season. Cutting can also be effective in eventually killing the plants.*

Covering stands of this plant with heavy sheets of black plastic or shade cloth can limit growth but shoots often peek out from great distances, so cutting is also necessary.

A glyphosate herbicide will work and a number of other chemicals are also effective against Polygonum cuspidatum. *Most are nonselective though, and valuable nearby plants are often in danger.*

Sheep Sorrel

Sheep sorrel (*Rumex acetosella*) should never be confused with the real cooking sorrel (*R. scutatus*) because the first is a forceful weed and the second a chosen crop. Even if it isn't growing nearby to your abode, sheep sorrel is doing well in over forty of the United States, not to mention Canada. It's known for a sour taste, the result of high levels of oxalic acid in the plants. Too much of this chemical is poisonous, both to animals and humans.

It's a perennial with slender rootstocks, growing about a foot high, and having very distinctive arrowhead-shaped leaves and clusters of tiny orange-yellow flowers (male) or red-orange flowers (female), with male and female flowers on separate plants. The flowers appear at the tips of the stalks. Fruits are a shiny golden brown.

Sheep sorrel is fond of acid soil, especially soils low in nutrients. Look for plants on the edges of roads, old fields, and abandoned land.

The perennial creeping rhizomes make it a persistent noxious weed and it's labeled as such in twenty states. But it does act as a measure for the quality of your own garden soil.

Method of Removal: *Pulling up sheep sorrel doesn't work for long because of the regeneration of its rhizomes. One method is to improve the quality of your soil by adding humus and compost. The better the soil quality, the more sheep sorrel fades away. Before seeds form, try repeated mowing since this eventually weakens the plant. Spot applications of a glyphosate herbicide also works.*

Yellow or Curly Dock

Here's another member of the buckwheat family, again in the genus of *Rumex,* and a larger weed than the above sheep sorrel. Docks are usually described as coarse weeds. The name *dock* is very old and refers to the resemblance of this plant's taproot to the solid part of an animal's tail (and dock is still in use as a word describing the removal or cutting short of a dog's tail). Docks are of European origin and came over with the first settlers, centuries ago.

Yellow dock (*Rumex crispus*) is a perennial with a large and tuberous root system. The waving and twisted leaves can reach a foot in length, arranged alternately up the stem. Plant height can be up to four feet. Branched flower spikes bear hundreds of little reddish or greenish flowers without petals and one mature plant can easily produce up to 50,000 seeds to spread about the land. Fruits are seedlike and are enclosed within three little wings. These plants make great additions to dried-flower arrangements.

The broad-leafed or bitter dock (*R. obtusifolius*) differs in having alternated leaves that are heart-shaped with reddish veins. The leaves of this plant have a soothing effect on skin burns caused by stinging nettles.

Both of these plants can be noxious weeds, forming large colonies and crowding out valuable native species.

Method of Removal: *Remove seedling plants upon their first appearance. Never let them go to seed. Regularly mow or cut off at*

*ground level, but be persistent because they often resprout. Root
pieces will also regrow.*

Sour Grass or Upright Yellow Sorrel

The wood sorrel family has a number of charming wildflowers and some tenacious weeds. High on the list of
weeds is sour grass or upright yellow sorrel (*Oxalis stricta*),
or as it's called in older books, *Oxalis europaea*. This species
name does not signify origins because sour grass is an
American native.

These weeds are basically perennial, although sometimes they will act like annuals. They are ubiquitous plants
being found throughout the eastern United States, up into
Canada, and out West, too. Sour grass is found in open
fields, lawns, abandoned land, greenhouse floors, and
woodland borders.

Plants are usually less than twenty inches in height
and may recline (in botany, a reclining plant is termed
decumbent) or stand erect. From a perennial taproot,
slender, slightly hairy, light-green stems grow alternate
leaves, each divided into three heart-shaped leaflets, almost like a cloverleaf. The leaves are creased and actually fold up at night. Bright yellow flowers have five
petals, are about a half-inch wide, and plants continue to
bloom from late spring to early fall. Seeds are contained
by an elongated capsule, which sends them flying when
it opens.

Method of Removal: Pull up small plants by hand, trying to get them before they set seed. As you improve garden soil, the sorrels will go on the decline. You can try a glyphosate herbicide during active growth, but sorrels are notoriously difficult to kill.

Horse Nettle

The horse nettle (*Solanum carolinense*) is not related to the true nettles. It's considered, by some, to be an attractive plant, by others, a weed. Other common names include bull nettle, Devil's tomato, and apple of Sodom.

It's an American native plant, found from eastern Canada, south to Florida, and west to Texas. Plants generally grow in waste places, abandoned fields, and old gardens.

Branching stems reach heights of about four feet and are adorned with star-shaped hairs as well as prickles. Three- to five-inch leaves are elliptical, rough, coarsely lobed, and again, covered with prickles. Five-petalled flowers are violet, blue, or rarely, white. The petals surround a yellow cone. Fruits are yellow, tomato-like berries, less than an inch in diameter.

The horse nettle's prickles are a nuisance, but because these plants are one of the hosts for the Colorado beetle, they should be removed for this reason alone.

Method of Removal: This plant is a toughie to eradicate. Remember to wear sturdy leather gloves when handing this plant since the prickles can get to be rather intense. Usually deep hoeing is needed. Or pull up young plants before the taproots get started. You can also try a herbicide on the weed's cut-off trunk.

Common Dandelion

What well-known plant, brought to America by early colonists from Europe, has a thick, almost black taproot that produces a rosette of long jagged leaves, each leaf so constructed that all the rain falling on this plant goes to the center, then on to the root, while each leaf is cut into great jagged teeth, some pointing out and some pointing in, and—to an active imagination—look like teeth? (Hint: Some plant observers have thought that these "teeth" bear a resemblance to those of a dog or even better, a lion, hence the original popular name, *dent de lion,* French for "lion's tooth.")

Of course, it is the ubiquitous dandelion (*Taraxacum officinale*), one of the planet's most famous and useful weeds.

The genus *Taraxacum* is derived from the Greek word *taraxos,* meaning "disorder" and *akos,* meaning "remedy." Other common names for this plant include swine's-snout, priest's-crown, wet the beds, lion's tooth, puffball, blow ball, Pu Gong Ying (Chinese), pee-in-the-bed, and wild endive. Some authorities have refined the lion's teeth analogy and suggested that the puffy yellow flowers might be compared to the golden teeth of the heraldic lion. Some maintain that the common name refers instead to the whiteness of the root, calling it a lion's tooth.

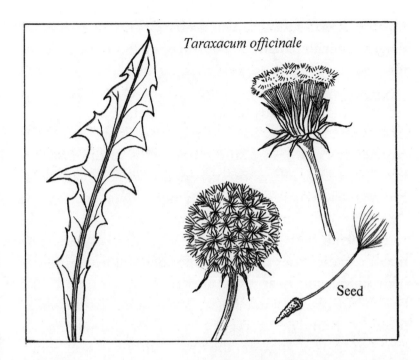

Taraxacum officinale

Seed

No matter how you name it, though, this is a very popular plant that receives both good and bad press. To people reveling in the purest of lawns, dandelions are a menace that requires the expenditures of vast amounts of time and energy spent keeping these weeds under control. To those who delight in the leaves as a great salad addition (young leaves make delicious sandwiches, the tender leaves being laid between slices of thin bread and butter, then sprinkled with salt or pepper), dandelion season is eagerly awaited every year.

The dried leaves of the dandelion are also used as an ingredient in many digestive beers (so popular in

Europe), and some folks will remember the popularity of dandelion wine, made by pouring a gallon of boiling water over a gallon of flowers, adding ingredients such as sugar and yeast, then bunging up the mixture for chilly summer nights. The roots of the dandelion are collected in autumn, roasted, and then ground to make dandelion coffee. It is also one of the bitter herbs of the Passover feast. And remember, too, that dandelions provide food for many wild animals such as bees, deer, geese, and rabbits.

Dandelions are widely distributed perennial weeds. The mature plant arises from a strong, deep taproot and has no visible stem. Leaves are clustered in a rosette at the base of the plant. Dandelions can reproduce from seed almost year-round or can regrow from their taproots. Flower heads are borne singly on the tip of a three- to twelve-inch long hollow stalk, are bright yellow, one to two inches across, and consist of petal-like ray flowers. The bristles on the seeds can clog cultivation equipment.

There's a lot of nectar in a dandelion blossom and watchful eyes will note that many little flies and larger bees flock around the blossoms. Observers have counted no less than ninety-three different insect types stopping off for a snack.

These blossoms are very sensitive to weather and when rain threatens, all parts of the head close up tight and around late afternoon, the flowers will also close to protect their contents for the next day's visitors.

When the flowers mature and the petals fall, the withered flower (or "swine's-snout") becomes a large ball of gossamer silk as plumed seeds fly off in all directions to start new plants in abandoned fields, and other people's lawns. Because of the many seeds that blow in from outside your property, nothing you can do will totally and permanently eliminate dandelion problems. However, you can greatly reduce the number of dandelions and other weeds that are able to take root in your yard by helping your grass plants to develop deep, healthy root systems that can compete well with weeds. In nature, grasses are more competitive than most weeds, especially annual weeds and perennials with roots that do not grow as deeply as healthy grass. Good watering, mowing, and soil care practices can help a great deal.

Method of Removal: *Young dandelions pull up easily if you twist as you pull. Grasp the plant below the leaves, at ground level, and twist while slowly pulling upward. You can also dig them up with a long, skinny "dandelion digger" with a forked tip. And use the same digger to get rid of other taproot weeds.*

Stinging Nettle

We've run up against a few weeds that are dangerous, if not downright unpleasant, to touch. Here's another, known quite properly as stinging nettle (*Urtica dioica*).

Nettles are herbaceous perennials commonly found growing in moist ground at the edge of woodlands, on abandoned farmland, wasteland in general, and along the edges of small streams and wooded creeks. They often form large colonies and crowd out other, more valuable, native plants.

These unpleasant-to-touch plants have a very long history and among the most interesting uses was one employed by Roman soldiers, who upon arriving in the chills of Britain (wearing short battle-skirts or above-the-knee tunics) would rub nettles on their legs to generate warmth— a tough way of keeping warm. Nettles have also been traditionally used as medicinals and cooked as vegetables in soups and stews.

Tough and straight stems grow about five feet high from fibrous roots below. They are covered with stinging bristles. Opposite leaves are egg-shaped, toothed, and tapered at the tips. There are also stinging cells on the leaf undersides. Tiny green flowers droop in branched clusters arising from the leaf axils.

The stinging cells act just like tiny hypodermic needles. When they touch the skin, little bulbs that contain several irritating chemicals (including formic acid, the same chemical used by ants) are released. The result is an immediate burning sensation.

Time is the antidote to burning. And keep in mind, once burned, twice shy.

Method of Removal: *Use caution whenever you come up against a clump of nettles. Remember to keep cats and dogs away,*

too. To remove them, cut them off at the ground level, and let them
dry. Once the stems and leaves are dry, they no longer sting, and
the remains can be raked up and taken to the compost heap.

Myrtle or Periwinkle

I would never have imagined that one day I would include
myrtle or periwinkle (*Vinca minor*) in a list of invasive
weeds. My first introduction to this plant came when I visited an old graveyard in the Catskill Mountains, in which

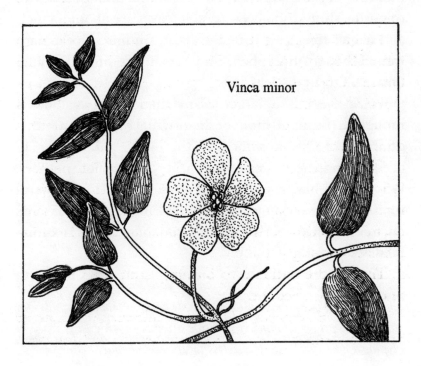

Vinca minor

the last person had been buried before the Civil War. Twining around the gravestones, a very healthy planting of myrtle sported glossy green leaves, and on that spring day, sparkling blossoms of periwinkle blue. The original plants were brought over from Europe and England as reminders of home, medicinal herbs, and to be planted in cemeteries.

Vinca minor, a member of the Dogbane Family, is a perennial, evergreen herb with erect flowering stems from six to eight inches tall, and trailing non-flowering stems that root at the nodes. The stems contain milky latex. The opposite, shiny, usually evergreen leaves are about an inch and a half long and round-ovate in outline. Flowers are funnel-shaped, five-lobed, and vary from violet to blue, borne singly in the leaf axils.

Vinca major is a larger plant than *V. minor*, and is thought to be an offshoot of the original myrtle, but with a doubling of chromosomes. Of the two, it's the more aggressive and the bigger problem. It's a native of southern Europe and has naturalized in areas of the United States where winters are mild. Once established, it soon crowds out native plants and unlike *Vinca minor*, allows no competitor to stand.

Method of Removal: *The only way to safely rid yourself of either type of myrtle is to remove the plants by hand or mow them down, close to the ground. The leaves have a waxy coating that repels a glyphosate herbicide so it's useless to attempt chemical control.*

The Pleasures and Pains of Moss

I live next door to a great garden that was first planted back in the 1950s and developed for the next thirty-five years. Over almost ten acres, Doan Ogden grew thousands of species of native plants, exotic plants, and trees.

One of the highlights is a Japanese-style garden, where instead of lawn, moss covers all, shaded here and there with old maple trees.

At any time of the year, it's beautiful—and maintenance is simplicity plus. All that's required is to rake autumn leaves off the moss within two or three weeks of their falling. That prevents the moss from going into a state of hibernation, whereupon it turns brown. Without the leaf cover, the moss stays a beautiful bronze-gold all winter long.

But if you would rather have lawn, then what's a gardener to do?

First, ask yourself why moss is moving in and grass is moving out. Well, remember, moss thrives in areas where grass is fighting for existence. Usually the soil that supports moss is acid, highly compacted, poorly drained, and infertile. And, too, grass likes sunlight while most of the mosses prefer shade.

To get rid of moss, loosen the plants with a metal rake and remove them. Aerate compacted soils. When growing in small patches on bricks or tiles, try one of the moss-killing soaps.

Then correct the problems that are causing poor grass growth so that the grass will better compete with the moss:

- To cut acidity, add limestone as necessary. Low soil pH can also encourage moss growth. PH tests are simple to use and you can do the tests on your own using materials available from yard and garden centers.
- Improve drainage to get rid of excess moisture.

12

Weedy Vines

Exotic vines are some of the worst invaders of our homes, pastures, fields, and woodlands because they often form infestations so thick that only brave explorers with machetes or flamethrowers could penetrate their growth. The infamous kudzu and the Japanese wisteria are fine examples of vines that can eventually topple forests and, in time, destroy everything they touch.

The Five-Leaf Akebia

As a garden writer I've often written nice things about plants that I later found to be slightly dangerous to the world around us and definitely not living up to their initial press.

Such a plant is the five-leaf akebia or chocolate vine (*Akebia quinata*), a woody vine flourishing in the temperate regions of eastern Asia, quite at home in much of the United States, and actively pursuing my garden.

It grows either as a twining vine or vigorous ground-cover with slender, rounded stems that begin as green but ripen to brown upon maturity. The palmate (like a hand) leaves of akebia alternate along the stem and are divided into five, or sometimes fewer, approximately equal parts called leaflets, whose small stems meet at a central juncture. Individual leaflets are generally an elongated oval in shape, about three inches long.

The flowers are an unusual chocolate-purple color and fragrant (mostly in the evening), about an inch across, and appear in late March to early April, when they are often hidden by new foliage. The fruits are purple-violet, flattened sausagelike pods, up to four inches in length, ripening in late September to early October. The inside of the pod has a whitish pulpy core with many tiny black seeds. Five-leaf akebia is deciduous in cooler climates but may remain evergreen in warmer regions, such as Louisiana.

Five-leaf akebia was brought to the United States in 1845 as an ornamental and has since naturalized in the warmer climates. It grows quickly and if left unmanaged, begins to smother plants at ground level, then spreads upward.

The vines are found in sixteen states in the eastern Unites States, from Michigan to Connecticut, and south to Georgia. Akebia is shade and drought tolerant and can invade many types of habitats.

Method of Removal: *Pulling up the vines by hand can control small collections of five-leaf akebia. Alternatively, you can cut* *them back with a mower, remembering to repeat the actions a number of times in the season. Vines can be dug up or if that's not possible, use a glyphosate herbicide.*

Porcelain Berry

Porcelain berry (*Ampelopsis brevipedunculata*) is on wanted posters as one of the top twenty invasive plants in New York State—and they're careful about what they feature on such a list.

A native of northeast Asia, the vine was once classified as a member of the ivy family, then it was shifted to the grape family, and finally in 1803, the genus *Ampelopsis* was created. It's a deciduous vine related to the wild grape, with green, lobed leaves that are hairy on the underside. It's the kind of a vine that nurseries often call "vigorous"— so you know it grows quickly.

The flowers are insignificant but upon maturity the plants produce large quantities of very attractive fruits with the color of pale blue porcelain. They eventually turn sky blue.

Porcelain berry will vine just about anywhere, especially in moist shady thickets. At first, in our garden, I found it quite beautiful as it rambled in and out of a very old yew hedge. But soon there were more vines than yews. Then I found that birds eat the berries and soon seedlings were everywhere.

The great press it receives as a landscape plant should be a clue that once settled in, it's a problem. It's disease and insect resistant, and quickly forms a living rug that not only cuts down on light but as rain falls on the leaves, it ranges far and wide before getting to the dry earth below.

Method of Removal: *Whenever possible, hand-pull seedlings. With patience, gloves, and a sharp pair of pruners, you can cut back a lot of vine, and then brush the cut ends with a glyphosate herbicide.*

Oriental Bittersweet

Like most of the invasive plant species we're battling today, oriental bittersweet (*Celastrus orbiculatus*) was purposely brought to America, and only later did gardeners discover its destructive potential.

Oriental bittersweet vine (an Asian native) was first introduced to North America in 1879 as an ornamental. It was close in appearance to our native bittersweet (*C. scandens*), which was once very common but is now difficult to find.

Make no mistake about it: This is a pernicious vine that ranks right up there with Japanese honeysuckle (*Lonicera japonica*), poison ivy (*Rhus radicans*), and Japanese wisteria (*Wisteria floribunda*). It produces far more fruit that the native bittersweet, so birds have more of it to eat and more of its seeds to spread.

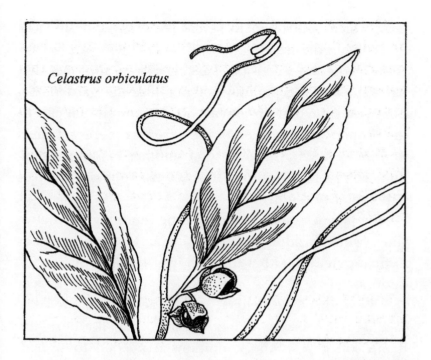

Celastrus orbiculatus

And spread it did! The vines are now found from New York, east to the ocean, and south to the Carolinas, and west to Illinois.

Oriental bittersweet is a deciduous perennial that begins as a softly twining vine. With age the vines become woody, grow up to four inches in diameter, and actually produce spiral indentations around, then over, the branches of the host bush, tree, or shrub. Rounded leaves have a fine-toothed margin and appear alternately along the stem. Clusters of small greenish flowers emerge from leaf axils. When mature, green to yellow globular fruits appear, which split open to reveal red-orange, fleshy arils that contain the seeds.

As I write, my wife is out hacking away at the vines that have entered the pathways of our lakeside garden, because, over the past three years, we've ignored that part of the property, and worked in the perennial border. Unless we remove them, they will soon smother existing vegetation, completely covering the victims, robbing them of light, water, and nutrition.

The Japanese species seems to be replacing our native vines (which produce fewer berries, and only on the ends of the branches), either through hybridization or by competition.

Like kudzu (see below), people actually planted the Japanese bittersweet as an erosion control where the damp soil gave it the conditions it needed to spread. Flower arrangers love them as well. Let's not forget all the tossed-out arrangements that went to the city dump or the local landfill, where the birds found the berries—and now look!

The vines do well at the edges of woodlands, in coastal marshes, and open fields. Their tolerance to shade makes them especially damaging to the forest understory.

Method of Removal: *Where practical, and always in the spring before flowers and fruits develop, gloved hands can pull up young vines or cut them with sharp tools. Wind the vines up into wreaths and put them in plastic lawn bags for removal to the dump or find a remote place on your property, and let them bake*

*in the hot summer sun. When stems are cut as close to the ground
as possible, brush the stumps with a glyphosate herbicide.*

Japanese Honeysuckle

Upon hearing a poetic line like "honeysuckle vines round my
heart," most gardeners will respond with invectives. If you
thought bush honeysuckle was a problem, wait until you confront the Japanese honeysuckle (*Lonicera japonica*).

As did many floral invaders, Japanese honeysuckle entered the country as a landscape plant, specifically settling
in on Long Island, New York, back in 1806. The even more
destructive cultivar known as Hall's honeysuckle arrived in
Flushing, New York, in 1862.

Neltje Blanchan, writing in *Nature's Garden* (New York:
Doubleday, Page & Co., 1904) describes the delicious
scent of the flowers, but notes that vines have "freely escaped from cultivation from New York southward to West
Virginia and North Carolina." A few years later the plants
arrived in the Deep South where they were described as "a
network of tangled cords that covers the ground wherever
this ruthless invader gets a foothold."

In North America, *Lonicera japonica* has few natural enemies and, once established, is difficult to control. Today
the vines are found throughout the North and Southeast,
with the exception of Maine, New Hampshire, and parts of
Kentucky. They are now spreading west to conquer Texas
and Oklahoma.

Japanese honeysuckle is a climbing or trailing vine with hairy stems when young. Older stems develop peeling bark. The medium-green, glossy, semi-evergreen leaves are opposite on the stems. Flowers appear on new wood, bloom in pairs, and are usually white, occasionally pink, and turn yellow with age. The fruits are shiny black berries. Birds eat the fruits.

The other problem vine honeysuckles are *Lonicera japonica* var. *halliana*, and *Lonicera japonica* var. *chinensis*. *L. japonica* var. *halliana* is distinguished from the species by its pure white flowers, which still fade to yellow with age, and its more vigorous growth. *L. japonica* var. *chinensis* has purple, essentially glabrous leaves, red flowers, and a more limited range than the species, so far being limited to New Jersey and Pennsylvania.

Because the vines adapt to many soil types and do well in full sun to dappled shade, they have not only invaded fields, forest clearings, and floodplains, but also have attacked the edges of woodlands. With the complexity of wires found in complicated electronic circuits, nothing escapes their clasping grip. Make no mistake: they can actually engulf small shrubs and trees.

Method of Removal: *Pull up seedlings by hand. When cutting vines back to rescue engulfed trees and shrubs, remember that cut vines can resprout. Therefore, trace the vine back to the ground and brush the cut ends with a glyphosate herbicide. Herbicides are best when applied after the first killing frost.*

Japanese Climbing Fern

The Japanese climbing fern (*Lygodium japonicum*) was first noticed in Hawaii back in 1936 when it was found growing in an old garden. Sometime during the last century, it was introduced into Florida, where it's become a pernicious weed. Recently the Florida Exotic Pest Plant Council has declared the Japanese climbing fern one of the worst invasive pests to arrive in that state.

Although freezing kills back the fronds, the rhizomes can survive some cold, thus they are spreading to South Carolina, Georgia, Alabama, Mississippi, and Louisiana.

A lacy plant with bright green leaflets, the fern blade's midrib actually winds around stems and branches of woody plants. The delicate ferny appearance belies the fact that these creepers easily climb trees and shrubs, where they form dense clumps, the stems twining in and out, eventually blocking out the sunlight. In addition, these mats can bring fires from ground level to the tree-tops.

Method of Removal: *You must bend down and cut away the fronds, pulling the rhizomes out of the soil. According to the Nature Conservancy, a mixture consisting of fifteen percent triclopyr and eighty-five percent of an oil surfactant has been used to spray the vines when up in the trees. Recently a foliar rust fungus was found to infect the ferns so there is some hope in developing a biological control.*

English Ivy

Originally from Eurasia, common English ivy (*Hedera helix*) was introduced into America way back in early colonial days as a landscape plant. Many gardens in my area of western North Carolina were originally planted with common English ivy (*Hedera helix*) as a ground cover and an alternative to cutting lawns.

It was a gigantic mistake. Today as you drive along the residential areas of many cities—from Atlanta, Georgia, up to towns in southern Pennsylvania—you will see ivy-covered trees rising up from green seas of ivy leaves, evergreen and impervious to almost everything that can be tossed its way.

When first planted, ivy is a crawling groundcover with the leaves resembling the ivies sold in small pots at nurseries. But after some ten or fifteen years, the vine begins to mature, and the leaves change to resemble a goose foot. Stems look for places to climb, and you soon have an arboreal shrub that will flower (small clusters of greenish-white or off-yellow flowers), then fruit with small seed-filled berries, like lackluster grapes.

Some plants, often spring ephemerals, will continue to exist in ivy patches, but most other plants will not.

The vines will not kill trees by strangulation (as many horticulturists warn), because the clinging stems rest on the surface of the bark, expanding out as the trunk grows. But if, in their climbing, they reach injured or weak branches, the extra weight of water, ice, or snow on the ivy leaves can be enough to cause the limbs to break and fall.

If you do want the ivy look for your lawn, be sure and look for newer cultivars, often with attractive variegations, that will not take such a choke hold on your property.

Although rare, some people suffer from contact dermatitis when their skin comes into contact with ivy sap. While not strictly poisonous, if eaten, the berries can cause gastric upset and diarrhea.

Method of Removal: *Forget about applications of herbicides since the waxy covering on ivy resists just about everything. Resign yourself to cutting the stems as they leave the soil for the tree trunks; the leaves quickly brown and will eventually fall from the now dead vines. Pull up the vines from the ground, winding them around your arms as you would a garden hose.*

Kudzu: The Black Belt Plant

Some years ago one of the greatest plant pests in the Southeast traveled thousands of miles and made ready to carpet any land to which it could put a root.

Its common name is kudzu (*Pueraria lobata*) and it's visible when driving back roads or even along the interstates. In fact, it's ubiquitous almost anywhere below the Mason-Dixon Line (and there are new reports of it being spotted in southern New York State and Connecticut). Wherever you amble along in the Carolinas, in Georgia, or as far north as southern Pennsylvania, you will spot tangled

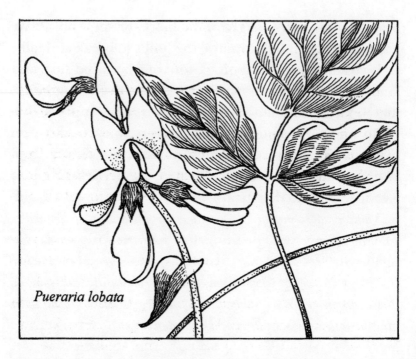

Pueraria lobata

masses of vines producing hordes of Gordian knots just the other side of the ditches.

These chlorophyll cords will clamber up steep cliffs and flow through the woods with ease, covering telephone poles, woodlots, cornstalks in the fields, and junk cars; it will wind through the front and out the rear of abandoned farmhouses and barns—in fact just about anything that moves slower than the U.S. mail.

Many cartoons have been drawn in jest, cartoons that show a farm couple on the front porch at 9:00 A.M., with the slimmest tendrils of kudzu sneaking in the back door and, by noon, they are embalmed in a tightly woven blanket of green.

It's kudzu on the move!

If you're looking for an approach to almost-instant topiary, kudzu is the answer. I have before me a black-and-white photo of some twenty trees—well over sixty feet high—entirely covered with this vine. It has flowed from branch to branch and transformed the whole affair into something resembling a menagerie of unidentified animals, all sitting up.

This member of the pea family is a semi-woody perennial vine. Its deciduous leaves are alternate and compound, with three broad leaflets that can grow as wide as four inches across. Leaflets are usually deeply lobed with hairy margins. Borne in long hanging clusters, kudzu's highly fragrant flowers appear in late summer and are about half an inch long. They are soon followed by brown, hairy, flattened seed pods, each of which contains three to ten hard seeds.

Vines will usually not flower the first year from seed but are still valuable as a temporary screen or arbor plant growing up to fifteen feet in one northern summer, but note, only in USDA Zone 4 or below should they even be attempted; anywhere else, eschew this plant.

But hang on. Researchers at Duke University are now predicting that the plant that ate the South will now stretch across state lines and as global temperatures rise in the twenty-first century, kudzu will, too. "In the future," said Boyd R. Strain, a botany professor, "with climate changes coming on, we are very concerned about its spread. The limits it now has are climate-controlled, and it may migrate to the North as the climate changes."

These black-belt champs of the vine world came from Korea and China. The genus, *Pueraria*, was named in honor—doubtful at best—of Marc Nicolas Puerari (1776–1845), a Swiss botanist. The species was originally named *lobata*, referring to the lobed leaves, but was recently changed to *montana* (for mountain). Its local name in Japan is *kuzu*.

Believe it or not, this vivacious and vicious vine once had a value to the Japanese. During the third or fourth century, weavers in Japan used kudzu to produce a fiber that was woven into a tough fabric prized by the ancient warrior class. Today, they probably have their own reservations about kudzu.

Kudzu has medicinal uses as well. The Chinese use a root tea for headaches, diarrhea, and gastroenteritis in general. A flower tea is reputed to help reduce stomach acidity, and it's also reputed to help over-zealous imbibers recover from a drunken state.

Kudzu has also been a foodstuff for thousands of years: The leaves can be eaten as a vegetable while the roots are a source of a starch that is in every way as good as arrowroot. The Japanese use it when deep fat–frying daylily leaves. And not to be left behind, bees make great honey from kudzu blossoms (which smell just like Kool-Aid), and the blossoms can also be used to brew a tasty tea.

In 1876, kudzu gained entrance to America when plants were used to landscape one of the gardens at the Japanese Pavilion during the Philadelphia Centennial Exposition. At the century's turn, kudzu was discovered to be an excellent forage for cows, pigs, and goats, especially in the South where acidic soils and long periods of drought were not the best conditions for the available corn cultivars of that time. It's not as nourishing as corn, but bear in mind that once planted, it can be harvested two or three times a year and never requires seeding again.

Later—and here's American capital on the move—the railroad barons also found kudzu was perfect as a living cover for the erosion damage created as they dug and dynamited cuts and gullies through the mountains of western North Carolina, Georgia, and eastern Tennessee. After 1970 there was no stopping it!

Today, the distribution of kudzu in the United States extends from Connecticut to Missouri and Oklahoma, and south to Texas and Florida.

As far as propagation, kudzu has many methods up its vine. Although producing few fertile seeds, what a plant does produce will germinate. It's been suggested that one way the plants spread results from pods falling into creeks and streams, eventually landing on a fertile bank, where they sprout.

Vegetative reproduction occurs as trailing vines root at the nodes. These new root crowns mature and send out more vines. Reproduction also occurs from rhizomes that sprout new vines. From early August until frost, sugars produced in leaves are transported to roots and are stored as starch. Under good growing conditions, kudzu can develop into an impassable mass of vines.

Method of Removal: *So how do you get rid of it? If the infestation is small, it can be done. Hack back to the place where the stem is level to the ground. You must do this continually for a couple of years.*

You can also apply a glyphosate herbicide to the cut ends. There are effective herbicides, but gardeners must bear in mind chemicals will not succeed without outside help. It can literally take years to kill a well-established vine. And remember, if the vine is on yours and a neighbor's property, you must work together in the scheme of eradication.

It should be noted that a herd of goats will also do an effective job of pruning. Their continued nibbling will weaken the roots, depriving them of food, and eventually the vines will die.

Mile-a-Minute Vine

Mile-a-minute (*Polygonum perfoliatum*) appears to grow that fast. Also called devil's-tail-tear-thumb, this annual herbaceous, trailing vine is another terror from the buckwheat family, originally hailing from India to eastern Asia, China, and the islands from Japan to the Philippines, as well as Nepal, Burma, Manchuria, Korea, Taiwan, and the Malay Peninsula.

Another attack from a Japanese native, the first records of mile-a-minute in North America cite Portland, Oregon (1890), and Beltsville, Maryland (1937). Neither of these sites established permanent populations of the species.

However, the introduction of mile-a-minute in the late 1930s to a nursery site in York County, Pennsylvania, did produce a successful population of this plant. It is speculated that the seed was spread with rhododendron stock. The nurseryman involved was so interested in the vine, its seeds were allowed to mature and were soon spread by birds, ants, and rodents that ate the fruits. From 1981 to 1989, mile-a-minute expanded from five Pennsylvania counties to eleven.

Plants have reddish stems, armed with hooks or barbs that point to the ground and hooks are also found on the leaf undersides. The light green leaves are shaped like equilateral triangles and alternate along the delicate and narrow stems. You'll also find distinctive circular, cup-shaped, tubular sheaths called ocreas, structures found in many polygonums, located near the leaf stems. Small, white, and inconspicuous flowers spring from these ocreas, later turning into metallic blue segmented fruits. Within each segment lies one glossy black seed.

Mile-a-minute weed grows quickly, rapidly running over everything in sight, including other vegetation. This results in the threatened plants losing valuable light and limiting their photosynthetic efforts, often resulting in death.

Naturally, infestations of mile-a-minute weed often attack native plant species often eliminating rare plants in natural areas. Because of this speedy growth, it has the potential to be a problem to nurseries and in horticultural crops where regular tilling is not practiced.

Mile-a-minute weed is currently found in New York, Pennsylvania, Maryland, Delaware, West Virginia, Virginia, Ohio, and Washington, D.C.

It is a temperate species with subtropical tendencies so it poses a major threat to areas where there's an eight-week period with sustained temperatures of 50°F or below. This, of course, covers a great deal of territory.

Look for this terror along the edges of wooded land, wetlands, streams, and uncultivated open fields. Although it's tolerant of some shade, it does require a dose of sunlight every day.

While mile-a-minute weed is killed by the lightest frost, it's also self-pollinating and produces a lot of fertile seed, without the assistance of bees and butterflies. And it produces a lot of seeds. These seeds are picked up by birds who carry them great distances. It's also noted that ants carry the seeds for short distances, seemingly attracted by a tiny food body found at the seed tip.

Water, too, moves many seeds since they can stay afloat for up to ten days. Because the spreading vines often hang over moving waters, the invasion goes on and on.

Method of Removal: Controls include physical, mechanical, cultural, and chemical. Pulling out seedlings by hand is best accomplished when they're young and the recurved barbs are still soft. When they are hard, you must use gloves. Just reel in the vines as if you were rolling up a garden hose. Then leave them to dry out.

Repeated mowing will prevent the plants from flowering, eliminating fruit formation and seeds.

Herbicidal soaps, available at most garden centers, will help to burn the new foliage of mile-a-minute. But you've got to keep up the applications because, unlike the glyphosates, soaps won't travel to the roots. Glyphosates are also usually effective.

Deadly Nightshade

A climbing member of the great tomato family, deadly nightshade (*Solanum dulcamara*) is also known as bittersweet nightshade, dulcamara, and felonwort. The vine came over from Europe with the early settlers. It's interesting to note that the dried fruits of *S. dulcamara* were found within the tomb of Tutankhamen.

Vines can grow up to ten feet. The leaves are usually over three inches long and have two basal lobes. The flowers are very attractive, consisting of drooping clusters of blue or violet, star-shaped blossoms, with a yellow beak in the center. The fruits or berries begin as a shiny green but soon turn a bright red.

Although it was first brought to this country as a medicinal plant, it should be remembered that all parts of deadly nightshade are poisonous and should be treated with care.

Method of Removal: Because this weed is a vine, removal is best achieved by cutting the stem off at ground level, thus letting the vine perish. Try to achieve this before the berries appear.

Poison Ivy

"Leaflets Three, Let Them Be" is one of those old saws that we first hear from a relative who's suffered from meeting this vine head on, or from Scout leaders during marches in the woods, or from savvy suburban and rural school-teachers who happen to live in areas where this vine grows well.

Hikers, home-owners, and gardeners usually meet three toxic members of the P. I. tribe: poison oak (*Rhus diversiloba*); poison ivy (*R. radicans* and *R. toxicodendron*), also called poison oak, cow-itch, and markry; and poison sumac (*R. vernix*), also called swamp sumac, poison elder, and poison dogwood. The botanical name of poison ivy has been *Rhus radicans* for decades, with *Rhus* being an ancient Greek name for the genus and *radicans* meaning rooting, and they certainly do. But it was recently changed to *Toxicodendron radicans*, which means poison tree that roots. It should be noted that the scientific names of all these plants' genus have been changed from *Rhus* to *Toxicodendron* but most books still use *Rhus*—and I will, too.

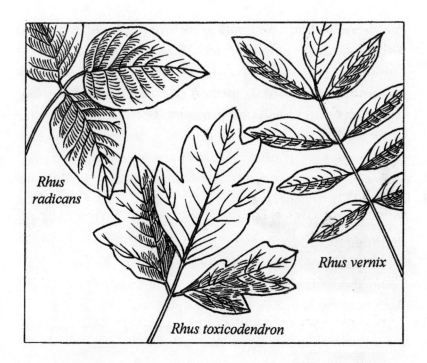

Rhus
radicans

Rhus vernix

Rhus toxicodendron

These poisonous plants are members of the cashew
family. All parts of each plant described below are poisonous to the touch. Yet, believe it or not, back in the mid-
1700s, poison ivy was once sold by the pot at Bartram's
Philadelphia Nursery. Everybody wanted the beauty of its
autumn foliage in their gardens.

Poison oak (*R. diversiloba*) grows as a shrub to eight feet
and often climbs wooden supports, either posts or trees.
The compound leaves grow in threes, are about three
inches long, and either toothed or lobed. The flowers

are greenish and the fruits are clusters of white berries. The plants are common from British Columbia to Baja, California.

Another poison oak species (*R. toxicodendron*) is basically a creeping shrub that grows to about six feet, bearing three leaflets, each lobed or bluntly rounded, and spreading by creeping runners. Flowers are greenish, blooming in panicles, and the fruits are white. It grows throughout eastern North America.

Poison sumac (*R. vernix*) is a shrub or small tree but is included with the others as a matter of convenience. Height is usually about twenty feet, leaves are compound (but grow with seven to thirteen leaflets instead of three), flowers are greenish, and the hanging bunches of fruit are greenish, too. The leaves turn a brilliant crimson in the fall.

With age, vines can get very thick. I've found noble vines over two inches in diameter, clinging to the sides of trees, notably apples. The amazing thing about this ivy is its ability to wander along the forest floor for years, appearing to be a rambling and weak-stemmed vine, acting as a groundcover and creeper. The infamous "three leaves" in this stage are rather small, usually under six inches, long, bright green—but still poison to the touch of most people. But suddenly it will start to climb a tree, producing a vine of such girth that Tarzan could probably swing on it if he was immune to the vine's deadly itch. The leaves can then reach ten inches in length and become quite attractive in their own right. Over many years the vines grow larger until they become as thick as a transatlantic cable. They have tiny rootlets on either side, wiry projections that work their way into the tree's bark giving added support to the vine, and giving them a decidedly hairy look. And they are strong.

On the plus side, poison ivy provides valuable winter forage for wildlife. The fruits are eaten by many birds, who suffer no ill effects. And if you have an area of wild garden where the ivy has vined up a tree and you can keep visitors away from it, let it be. For in the fall, the leaves turn a beautiful golden yellow; in fact, if the plant were not poison, we would all be growing it in the backyard.

The problem with these plants is that all parts of it—roots, stems, leaves, berries, and flowers—contain volatile oils that cause severe skin inflammation, itching, and blisters because they act on the histamine found in the cells of the human body.

American Indians rubbed leaves on an existing rash for treatment and homeopathic physicians use tiny doses to treat allergies, but the dose used is so small that only a trained physician can handle the job properly.

The rash that one gets from poison ivy is a reaction to a chemical in the sap called urushiol. Urushiol is rendered inactive by water, but the chemical can survive dormant for months or years on shoes or on clothing that hasn't been washed or on dead ivy roots buried in the ground. Reactions to urushiol are highly variable from person to person. Sensitive people will get a rash if they put on a patch with a one-thousandth of one percent solution of urushiol on it.

By the time the typical victim begins to itch, the urushiol is gone.

The skin that first contacts the sap and has the largest dose of the oil will usually break out with a rash the first time one is exposed to urushiol. Then soon after brushing against poison ivy, the victim can spread this oil by touch, and if the oil reaches the face, a rash can break out in hours (although even when directly exposed, the palm of the hand never reacts). The skin on the inner arm is also very tender, but on the thicker skin of the lower arm, the rash takes longer to develop. Sometimes a part of the body that has not been directly exposed will break out, usually because the skin has been sensitized by a previous attack.

Each year sees another batch of chemicals introduced to relieve the curse of poison ivy, so if you do get this curse, rather than scratching yourself to distraction, call your doctor or make a trip to the nearest pharmaceutical counter or drug store.

And woe to the person who burns the ivy and inhales the smoke. Never, never, burn any part of this plant. The irritant rides on smoke particles and the inside of your mouth, throat, windpipe, and lungs will react in the same way as the back of your hand. In fact, smoke from burned plant specimens more than 100 years old can still cause dermatitis, whether inside the body or out. Imported lacquerware is often coated with a finish that contains the Asiatic species (*Toxicodendron verniciflua*) and just touching the surface can provoke reactions in susceptible people.

There are a few chemicals that can kill poison ivy but one must remember that even a dead and dried plant can still irritate skin. The heavy, tree-climbing vines can be cut at the base but remember to wear gloves because the sap is the worst irritant.

Washing thoroughly with soap and water or swabbing the infected spots with alcohol within five to ten minutes of exposure usually (but not always) removes the oil-based irritant and generally prevents the rash. The flaw in that solution is that you don't always realize when you have been exposed. Many people are surprised when they break out in blisters and itch, not remembering when they were infected. And don't forget the dog or cat. If they wander through a patch and then you pet the animal, you will probably get it again.

The washing treatment, if done immediately, usually works on the rash but I've also been scarred by the thorns of poison ivy brambles. I really looked like one of the victims in a slasher horror film. This led me to trust the rumor that a gardener's life is not always a pleasant romp through a field of wildflowers but more often than not, akin to using a machete to make a path through the jungle.

Method of Removal: If pulling vines out of the garden, wear gloves and a long-sleeved shirt, remembering to wash all your

*clothes after use. The safest thing to do with the collected plants is
to let them air dry until dead and then bury them.*

*Glyphosate herbicides will kill poison ivy, and this method of
removal is very effective if you are only killing the plants and not
planning on gardening the area later. Remember, dead roots that
you find years later can still cause toxic reactions.*

*My advice is to buy a few giant packs of disposable rubber
gloves—the kind doctors and vets use and are sold at most drug-
stores—then wear long pants that reach down and over your shoe
tops plus a sweatshirt that covers your wrists with the ends tucked
under the gloves. Then stop every so often to change gloves, carefully pulling them off and replacing them.*

Chinese or Japanese Wisteria

There's a grove of southern yellow pines growing adjacent
to the Blue Ridge Parkway, just north of the Folk Art Center and south of Asheville, North Carolina. They've been
attacked by some Japanese wisterias (*Wisteria floribunda*)
and year-by-year, you can watch the vines get thicker and
thicker while the trunks begin to grow around them, an
action that will eventually lead to their death. For make no
mistake about the strength of non-native wisterias: They
have been known to bend stout pipes and ravage trellises
built to super specifications.

The exotic wisterias are now at home in much of the
United States; the Chinese wisteria arriving in 1816 and
the Japanese in the early 1930s.

Both the Japanese and Chinese wisteria (*Wisteria sinesis*) are beloved, exotic, showy in bloom, woody ornamental vines belonging to the pea family. Described as "vigorous" (a word that should alert all gardeners to its questionable habits), these vines have the ability to reach treetops, regardless of height, and eventually destroy all that they climb.

The compound leaves of the Japanese wisteria have up to nineteen leaflets while the Chinese have thirteen. Unlike our staid and respectful American wisteria (*Wisteria frutescens*), a native beauty that flowers in summer, oriental wisterias blossom in late spring with long hanging clusters of fragrant pealike blossoms in colors (depending on the species and the cultivar), ranging from white to violet to pastel purples. Fuzzy, about five-inch-long brown seedpods ripen in the fall.

The clasping stems of the exotic wisterias can have a diameter of almost fifteen inches, the Japanese species twining clockwise and the Chinese twining counterclockwise. Usually the vines spread with air-borne runners that quickly bend to the ground, and then root. Seeds will germinate in warmer climates but are killed by frost.

The exotic wisterias (not the native) are ruthless in their expansion and the clasping vines can literally choke a mature tree to death. Upon reaching the forest canopy, the wisteria leaves absorb the sun they love, and diminish the light for all the rest of the plants below.

Note: The American wisteria is a beautiful vine that doesn't sucker, has lovely blossoms of pale lilac, blooms in the late summer, and hugs a trellis with care. It is hardy to USDA Zone 5.

Method of Removal: Keep in mind that wisterias will continue to resprout as long as there is a food reserve left in the roots. Therefore, try to cut back the vines in late winter before they begin to grow, continuing to recut all summer. You can kill a vine by cutting it at the base, but caution is needed because the vine left encircling the tree will eventually girdle the trunk, killing the host unless removed. Brush the stump with a glyphosate herbicide.

13

Aquatic Weeds

J ust when you thought it would be safe to enter the water, you find out that weeds have invaded that domin-
ion, too. Check back in chapter 6 and you'll learn
that a number of weed seeds not only travel around on
land and in the air, but also by water. So even if you only
have a small backyard pond, you can suddenly find duck-
weed or parrot-feather or any number of aquatic weeds,
brought there by seeds clinging to a water bird's foot or a
frog's fin.

Aquatic Weed Control

If in doubt as to a plant's identity, collect a sample of the
offender, wrap it in wet paper towels, and in turn place
that in a sealed plastic bag. Then contact your local extension agent or state conservation department. After they
identify the species, they can offer recommendations for
specific control or removal methods. But, unfortunately,

because we are now dealing with water, unless your area is a small, enclosed pond, there are no satisfactory guarantees that any method of weed control will be effective over the long haul. And keep in mind that ponds are part of an open system. Whatever you put into the water will work its way downstream and could cause problems for neighbors down the line.

Read the label of any chemical that you consider using in water. Unless the label specifically states that a product is for killing aquatic weeds, pass it by. There is only one herbicide that I would ever feel even remotely comfortable using, and that is a glyphosate compound specially formulated for killing waterweeds. (To my knowledge, the only glyphosate-based product labeled for aquatic use is Rodeo®.) And never, never buy on the cheap. You might find a great bargain on imported sneakers but you get what you pay for when using commercial herbicides. And, again, remember to *always* read the product directions, *always* be careful, and *never* do anything but what is recommended on the label.

The following bits of advice are aimed at homeowners who are preparing to build a pond in their backyards. Before you pack up the shovels and stow away the leftover pond liner, consider the following:

- If the major portion of your pond is at least three
  feet deep, you prevent the foothold shallower depths

offer many weeds. However, steep banks can be haz-
ardous for swimmers, so use a gentle slope if you
plan on water activities.

- Draining a pond is a great way to get rid of invasive
  weeds. If you have a dam or spillway, it's possible to
  dry the invading weeds to death.

- Power-driven weed saws and cutters designed for underwater use are available.

- In lightly infested areas, hand-pulling weeds is still
  the best and surest way of gaining control of your
  pond.

- Aquatic weeds that die in the water decompose in the
  water, taking up valuable oxygen (especially if there
  are fish present). This often results in the growth of
  unwanted algae.

Water Hyacinth

Water hyacinths (*Eichhornia crassipes*) were imported from
South America as ornamentals back in 1884, whereupon
they immediately escaped from cultivation. They were
soon floating freely in lakes, rivers, bayous, and canals.
They are now a major pest throughout much of the inland
waterways of the Southeast and out West, too. They have,
in fact, become swimming kudzu.

They may be beautiful to look at as they blossom with
their very pretty lavender-purple flowers held high above
attractive leaves that float on the water's surface and their

dangling roots waving below, acting as water filters and spawning spots for pond life that shares the water. But, unfortunately, these lovely leaves and graceful roots transform into impenetrable mats of living plants that clog waterways, halt below-water motor boats in their tracks, and crowd out just about everything except themselves. Ultimately, water hyacinths build up and become some 200 tons of plant material covering one acre of water. And plants can double their mass in a little less than twelve days.

They multiply with runners that extend from the parent plants, which float because the base of each stem is a spongy mass of air pockets. Eventually, as the raft of plants gets thicker and thicker, air circulation is cut off and the water below begins to stagnate.

While Northerners can still buy the plants, in most southern states sale of water hyacinths is against the law.

Method of Removal: Forget about using herbicides on your own. The only way you can go the chemical route is by hiring commercially approved exterminators. However, for small infestations, the best thing to do is rake up the plants and haul them to the compost heap.

Brazilian Elodea or Giant Waterweed

First introduced as an aquarium plant, Brazilian elodea (*Elodea densa*) appeared on the market in the late 1800s. It was touted as being a great oxygenator, helping to replen-

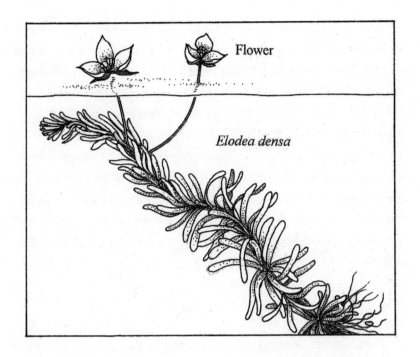

ish oxygen for needy tropical fish. The first plants to escape into our ecosystems were probably discarded by fish fanciers cleaning out their tanks. In the United States, this plant has run wild in fresh inland waters from Washington to Massachusetts, California, and Florida.

The narrow, filmy, bright green leaves are arranged in whorls of four on long stems up to thirteen feet long. Small white flowers with three petals form above the surface, standing above the water at least an inch or two. When used in an aquarium, stems are often tied in bunches.

Once they begin to grow in open water, they form dense mats that choke out native plants, get tangled up in fishing lines and boat propellers, and are just unpleasant to run into while swimming. According to published reports, an estimated 1,500 acre-feet of storage capacity were lost annually in Lake Marion, South Carolina, because of sedimentation due to Brazilian elodea.

Method of Removal: *For small infestations, you can gather the stems by hand but you must get every last piece. Another effective method of eradicaiton is to cover the plants with opaque black plastic because without light, they soon die. Before using herbicides, check with your extension agent.*

Horsetails

Horsetails (*Equisetum hyemale*), or—as they are sometimes called—"scouring rushes," are perennials that look as though they've come from prehistoric times; only somehow they shrunk in their travels. The name scouring rush refers to their use in old railroad days as a kind of always-at-hand Brillo®. Horsetails contain a great deal of silica and cooks of the line would use a handful of these plants to scour pots and pans after frying up eggs and bacon. When the chores were finished, they would toss the used stems out the window where they would promptly root in the railroad bed of gravel and stone.

Horsetails are perennials, growing about four feet tall, with their ribbed green stems shooting up from a creeping underground rhizome. The stems are made of many sections, each section between two and three inches long. Conelike caps produce spores, not seeds. The leaves have been reduced to very small black pennants that grow at the juncture where the stem sections meet.

Horsetails are extremely invasive and will form large colonies, usually growing alongside ditches, at the edge of old railroad beds, and on abandoned land in general.

Method of Removal: Because their stems are so tough and shored up with silica, a waxy coating, most herbicides are of little use. However, in her book Weeds: The Unbidden Guests in Our Gardens *(New York: The Viking Press, 1978), Mea Allen suggests another way to combat horsetails, "I have, however, heard of a cure: It is to sow the area with nasturtiums. These plants act as a smotherer and finally exterminator, for the horsetail cannot tolerate overshadowing competition." Somehow, I think you are further ahead by pulling up the stalks, grabbing them at the soil level, and doing it every time new shoots appear.*

Water Primrose

The water primrose (*Ludwigia uruguayensis*) is a perennial aquatic herb that grows in the shallows, usually at depths of less than three feet. It was introduced as an ornamental water plant in the mid-1950s. Today it's listed as a noxious weed in thirty-five states, throughout the Southeast and in California, Oregon, and Washington.

The smooth stems have a sparse coating of fine hairs, bear alternate, willowlike leaves that become rosettes of rounded leaves on the water's surface. Flowering stems can reach three feet above the surface. The flowers are bright yellow, followed by a cylindrical fruit. These water-weeds are not to be confused with our native ludwigia (*L. palustris*) since this species does not sprawl and bears tiny petal-less flowers in the leaf axils.

Water primroses are invasive plants that form tangled masses of vegetation that eventually crowds out native species. It is an extremely unpleasant partner in water-front activities.

Method of Removal: *Besides the time-honored method of cutting and raking, it's possible to kill a small infestation by covering the plants with an opaque plastic sheet.*

Parrot-Feather

Parrot-feather (*Myriophyllum brasiliense*) is named for the featherlike leaves that whorl gracefully about underwater stems. A native of the Amazon River in South America, the plants were probably imported in the late 1800s. Today, the plant has invaded most of the South, has traveled up the coast, and is found on the West Coast, too. You've seen the plants every time you've visited a pet store with tropical fish.

Parrot-feather has two kinds of leaves: submerged leaves a few inches long with many divisions, and above-water leaves with six to eighteen divisions per leaf. The emergent leaves can grow about a foot above the water's surface. Tiny inconspicuous white flowers are borne in the leaf axils of the emergent leaves.

This waterweed is responsible for a number of environmental threats. The plants can become so thick they cut off adequate life support to native plants that grow in deeper water, especially algaes that provide food for smaller species of aquatic animals. And worst of all, a screen of parrot-feather provides a perfect place for mosquito larvae to hide.

Method of Removal: *Parrot-feather leaves and stems have a thick waxy cuticle that resists herbicides. This coating also makes the plants unpalatable to fish as well. For small infestations, the homeowner must meticulously rake up the strands, making sure that every part of the weed is trapped. Investigations continue into a possible biological control. For large-scale infestations, contact your local extension agent or state conservation department.*

Eurasian Watermilfoil

Known as Eurasian watermilfoil or spike milfoil (*Myriophyllum spicatum*), this waterweed is now a major pest that forms large mats of intertwined vegetation, which cut down on available light for deeply submerged plants, harbors mosquito larvae, and easily tangles in boat engines and fish nets. Eurasian watermilfoil was introduced into the United States from Eurasia in the 1940s, as an aquarium plant. It most likely escaped into the natural environment when somebody cleaned out a fish tank. Plants are now found in every state east of the Mississippi and it was recently sighted in Colorado.

Stems grow to the water's surface and can reach lengths up to thirty feet, twisting in and out. Finely divided gray-green leaves grow in whorls along the stem, with twelve to sixteen pairs of again fine, thin leaflets about a foot long. Small yellow flowers are held above the water on short spikes. The fruit is a hard capsule containing four seeds.

Method of Removal: *For small infestations, the homeowner should use a hand-rake and carefully, repeat, carefully rake up the strands, making sure that every part of the weed is gathered. The best time is early summer when the plant growth begins to peak. Investigations continue into a possible biological control. For large-scale infestations, contact your local extension agent or state conservation department.*

Curly Pondweed

Until Eurasian watermilfoil hit the scene, curly pondweed (*Potamogeton crispus*) was the worst pondweed in many states, including much of the Midwest. Today it's found in forty-two states. Originally natives of Europe, the plants were introduced to the United States around 1879, imported as aquarium ornamentals.

These hardy perennials are attractive plants with stems of varying lengths up to twelve feet or longer, having three-inch-long slender leaves with attractive wavy edges and varying in color from green to a reddish brown. Flowers appear in elongated spikes held above the water. In nature, new plants can form under an ice cover and when the ice melts in spring, curly pondweed is raring to go. By midsummer it dies back, the decaying plant material providing water nutrients that often lead to ugly algal blooms and also a loss of dissolved oxygen.

Method of Removal: As with Eurasian watermilfoil, for small infestations, the homeowner must meticulously rake up the strands, making sure that every part of the weed is trapped. Investigations continue into a possible biological control. For large-scale infestations, contact your local extension agent or state conservation department.

Algae

Algae represent a large group of aquatic weeds that belong to the plant world but have few of the characteristics found in most plants. Whether floating on the top of the water, emersed (rooted in the soil below with tops above water), or submersed (rooted in the soil below with tops mostly under water), they often threaten the existence of aquatic installations—from hotels on the ocean to the old swimming hole to a backyard pond or a tropical fish tank.

Ranging from the microscopic cells that color water green to the 200-foot-long giant kelps of the Pacific Ocean, algae poses threats to swimmers, among them various kinds of dermatitis. Algae sometimes generates an incredibly smelly mess that winds up suffocating aquatic wildlife and driving people out of the area.

As with waterweeds, if in doubt as to an algae's identity, collect a sample of the offender then seal it in a waterproof plastic bag. Then, contact your local extension agent or state conservation department.

Method of Removal: One of the earliest chemicals used for aquatic algae control is copper sulfate (or copper-triethanolamine complex). Known as an algaecide, when it is added to pond water, you immediately know it because the water turns a vivid blue-green.

To attack algae growing on top of the water, copper sulfate can be used as a spray. For below-surface infestations crystals placed in a cloth bag and towed behind a boat until dissolved can be an effective control.

Store the chemical in a cool dry place, and be sure to keep containers closed. Avoid breathing any dust from copper sulfate because it not only irritates the skin but also causes severe eye irritation. Follow label instructions to the letter. Remember, if not properly handled, it's toxic to fish and to aquatic life.

14

Lawns and Weeds

There is a story, probably apocryphal, about two wealthy Americans touring a grand English estate.

"Goodness," said the wife as they trod the palatial lawn, "this grass is simply beautiful," and turning to the head gardener, she asked, "How in the world does one get a beautiful lawn like this?"

"Well, ma'am," he replied, "first you roll it for four hundred years."

Most of us are denied a head gardener, much less somebody to help with the lawn who knows the difference between a broad-leafed weed like a plantain or a garden hosta that is slightly out of place. When it comes to our lawns, we are usually on our own. The first thing we have to do is know our everyday lawn weeds who include dandelions, chickweed, plantains, wild onions, and all the other common invaders. These weeds have biological advantages over the grasses we plant for lawns; weeds have evolved to adapt to inhospitable soils, hot sun, and lack of water.

Lawn weeds are symptoms of an unhealthy lawn, but not the cause. Weeds march in when the grass roots are not vigorous enough to keep the weeds from spreading. Therefore, your first step in weed control is to determine why the grass is doing poorly. Does it need fertilizer? Does it need an application of lime to alter the pH? Have the kids compacted the soil with heavy foot traffic? Have you mowed the grass too short? Have you mowed the lawn too often? Correcting any of these problems increases your chance of improving the scene.

Once you have improved your lawn's health, you can check the type of weeds described in this book and choose the best method to get rid of them. If you do choose to use an herbicide, there are several general rules to follow:

1. Apply the herbicide when the weeds are growing well.
2. For best results, the temperature should be in the mid-70°F range.
3. Never use broadleaf weed killers in the summer heat of July and August.
4. If you choose a dry granular form of weed killer or one of the combination "weed 'n seed" varieties, make sure the grass is wet, not dry.
5. If you spray an herbicide, make sure it's a calm day. These weed killers are unable to differentiate between a weed and a beloved plant.

6. Choose a sunny day to spray.

7. Always read the label and always check to see that there is an 800 number to call if you run into problems. Wear adequate clothing, including gloves, and take care to protect your eyes.

Starting a New Lawn

If you really have a problem lawn that's almost too far gone to resuscitate, how about putting in a new lawn?

First, before one seed is sown, you must prepare the soil. Rent or buy a small rototiller and dig up the area dedicated to the new lawn. Then lay down a two-inch layer of composted manure (either cow or sheep) over the potential seedbed and rototill it again, mixing it all up.

Next, water the area making sure that the top two inches are moistened. The water will stimulate the germination of any weed seeds in the soil. For a week or two let the area alone until you spot a green fuzz of weed seedlings.

After a week or two has passed, rototill the area again, with the tillers set at a shallow setting, so you just turn over the weed seedlings and not go deep enough to stir up new weed seeds. Or, if you have strength, just hoe it up on the surface. If the new green growth is substantial, water again, and go through the process a second time, to force any remaining seeds into germination.

If you have a small lawn and a rototiller is not practicable, check the flame-killing weed equipment described in chapter 3. Small flamers use portable propane torches that are passed over the weeds, which kill them by boiling their sap, without even charring the plants. Once you've flamed the area, water as you did at the beginning, and wait for the second crop of weeds, and then flame them again.

After the second tilling or flaming, complete the soil preparation by raking in any additional nutrients that may be needed (see the extension agent for your area), and remove any rocks and clods.

Next level the soil, and sow grass seed according to instructions, raking it in lightly. Then apply half an inch of organic mulch and, finally, water again to moisten the lawn seed and stimulate germination. Be sure you select a grass variety suitable for your soil pH and your growing conditions.

Now don't get discouraged, but in addition to your new grass, a number of annual weeds will usually appear. Most will either die or be crowded out after several mowings. If, perchance, some of the uglier weeds like Canada thistle or field bindweed show up (courtesy of our fine feathered friends), see the listings for their particular species.

Recommended Lawn Grasses

Bent grasses (*Agrostis* spp.) are attractive in a lawn but require frequent mowing and thatch removal. The plants spread by stolons, grow well in humid locations, and thrive in the North. They are prone to problems when weather is hot and muggy, though, and they need regular watering and fertilizing. Velvet bent grass (*Agrostis canina*) is sometimes used for putting greens; redtop (*A. gigantea*) is used for both lawns and pastures; and colonial bent grass (*A. tenuis*) is also used for lawns. There are a number of cultivars on the market.

Buffalo grass *(Buchloe dactyloides [B. secundatum])* on the other hand, is represented by one species that is especially good in the dry, midwestern plains. The low-growing narrow, gray-green blades are less than an eighth-inch wide and form a thick sod that requires little mowing. They can be mixed with other grasses or used to cover dry, exposed banks.

Bermuda grass (*Cynodon dactylon*) is fast-growing, spreading by runners. Although attractive, it needs lots of care, including thatch removal. It needs full sun and is not hardy north of Tennessee. This grass is best for southern lawns.

Centipede grass (*Eremochloa ophiuroides*) is a medium textured, handsome, spreading plant that requires little maintenance. It prefers soil of poor to average fertility, with an acid pH; it does not do well in rich, alkaline soil. This grass can be difficult to grow and does best in the South.

Red fescue (*Festuca rubra*) is a fine textured grass, usually spreading by rhizomes. Well-suited to poor, dry, soil and dry, shady conditions, it will also grow well in sun.

Fescues do not thrive in hot, humid weather, but otherwise are very rugged.

Perennial ryegrass (*Lolium perenne*) makes a good starter grass, especially for covering bare soil. Fast growing, it quickly covers an area but, because it grows in bunches, it's a non-spreader. Unfortunately ryegrasses are not quite as hardy as bluegrass, and when used by themselves do not make really attractive lawns.

Annual ryegrass (*Lolium multiflorum*) is a fast spreader and, until there is time to seed a perennial lawn, can be used as a temporary groundcover.

Bahia grass (*Paspalum notatum*) is a medium textured grass with flat or folded blades that spread by runners. Not the best-looking lawn grass, but low in maintenance, it is adaptable to a range of conditions. It grows best in the South.

Kentucky bluegrass (*Poa pratensis*) is a beautiful, durable grass that recuperates well after winter, spreading by rhizomes. Both sun and shade varieties are available. It does well in northern lawns.

St. Augustine grass (*Stenotaphrum secundatum*) is a coarse textured plant that spreads quickly by runners. Although it grows well in the Deep South, it tolerates shade, but it is prone to thatch. (A variegated form, 'Variegatum', makes an excellent pot plant.)

Zoysia grasses (*Zoysia* spp.) are often the subject of full-page magazine advertisements and are billed as "miracle grasses." They resemble Bermuda grass but are slow-growing and can be difficult to establish. In spring, they are late in turning green but are attractive when the change occurs. They are very tough and durable, but because of their density, must be mowed with heavy-duty equipment. They are prone to thatch and are best for southern lawns.

Watering Schedules

I'm often asked about watering a lawn, especially now that around the country, water is getting more expensive.

The average lawn probably needs one to two inches of water every week, and when you do water, the soil should be moistened to a depth of between four and six inches.

But, as with everything else in the world, most people think that if a little water is good, more is better. Yet just as a lot of light watering will encourage weeds and shallow grass roots that easily burn on hot days, too much water will waterlog the soil, keeping oxygen away from the roots. Shallow roots are prime candidates for destruction, especially in drought conditions. Unless your lawn is on sandy and porous soil, it would be best to wait until the grass shows signs of wilting and then soak it with as much water as the ground will hold.

Gardeners should remember that only three-quarter-inch-diameter hoses deliver enough water pressure to properly operate most garden sprinklers. The sprinkler itself should release large drops of moisture, not a mist, because mist evaporates quickly and much of the water is lost before it reaches the ground.

The timing is important, too. The best times to water are early morning and early evening, to avoid the additional heat of the summer sun and the drying effects of daytime winds.

But how do you know that enough water has been used? Usually 0.6 inches of water will wet the soil to a depth of four inches, with sandy soils taking less and heavy clay soils needing more. To obtain a four-inch depth of moisture, the gardener would apply 528 gallons of water per 1,000 square feet. At a standard water pressure of 40 psi, using a three-quarter-inch, fifty-foot length of hose, the sprinkler would release 528 gallons an hour. In 45 minutes, 375 gallons would be released, thus wetting a completely dry soil to a depth of four inches.

Cutting the Lawn

In most cases, mow your lawn once a week, continuing to cut well into fall. The cutting height should be two and two-thirds of an inch at all times. By leaving the turf with a greater leaf surface, the plants hold more water and the leaves actually act as umbrellas, shading the roots from both the drying heat and evaporation of high summer, and also shading out the weeds.

It's possible to cut the lawn shorter in the early spring and in the fall, but keeping the height at three inches in the summer. Don't forget that a longer lawn is less likely to get weedy. And never remove more than one-third of the leaf blade at any one time since food is stored in the blades—removing these store houses is detrimental to the grass.

And, remember, a good mower has sharp blades. With today's rotary mowers, once the blade is dull, it doesn't cut but just beats the grass to death, leaving ripped and ragged tops that cause the plants to lose more water, become insect and disease prone, and look unsightly.

Finally, when cutting, remember that frequent mowing when the grass is one-third higher than the desired height, means grass clippings can be left where they fall to decompose and promote the health of the turf, as well as decrease trips to the compost heap or the local landfill.

In my lawns, we only bag the clippings that would fall directly in the pathways through the garden and around the front and back doors, so they are not tracked into the house. Everywhere else, they fall to the ground.

Mulching mowers are available, but we've found that most regular mowers that enable the user to close the side shoot, do a good job of returning the clippings to the mowed lawn where they quickly decompose. If you are using a bagging mower and you remove the bag, remember that the opening must be closed to prevent objects from flying out at a high speed. To avoid pile-ups of clippings, never mow the grass when wet and never remove more than one-third of the length of the grass blades in a single mowing. Keep in mind that clippings on the lawn do not contribute to thatch buildup. Thatch is made up of tough grass stems and roots and doesn't decompose quickly while grass blades are soft and quickly disappear.

Recent developments in clippings disposal include a grass clippings compost maker that will turn them into compost in less than thirty days. They can also be used to mulch garden beds.

De-thatch the lawn only when needed. Thatch is the buildup of a layer of plant debris that falls to the base of the sod before it can decay. Thatch makes it difficult (or impossible, if it gets bad enough) for water and fertilizers to penetrate the soil down to grass roots. There are machines and attachments for removing thatch. But earthworms are an excellent means of control—a good argument for avoiding the use of pesticides and herbicides at home.

Appendix I

Sources

When writing this book, I used a research tool that I would never have used a few short years ago. But the Internet, regardless of many crashing problems, has been a boon for checking facts and for finding out just how serious the spread of weeds in the United States has become.

The following sites are just a few of the sites searched over the past months of writing.

The Nature Conservancy is a nonprofit organization and the world's largest private international conservation group (www.nature.org). Their primary mission is providing members of The Nature Conservancy with sound management advice on invasive weed problems. The organization keeps files on more than 500 invasive plant and animal species. Go to: www.tncweeds.ucdavis.edu.

The Plant Conservation Alliance is a consortium of ten federal government Member agencies and over 145 nonfederal Cooperators representing various areas of the conservation field. PCA Members and Cooperators work collectively to solve the problems of native plant extinction and weeds. Go to: www.nps.gov/plants/index.htm.

The Natural Heritage Program represents a comprehensive effort to inventory and preserve the animal, plant, and natural community resources of the Commonwealth of Virginia and contributes to the recovery of vanishing species and communities. Go to: www.dcr.state.va.us/dnh.

King County, Washington, maintains a noxious weed control board and lists all Class A weeds that are notorious in the Northwest. Go to: www.splash.metroke.gov/wlr/lands.

The **University of California Statewide Integrated Pest Management Project** maintains a database with official guidelines for pests, pesticides, and non-pesticide alternatives for managing pests in homes and landscapes. Go to: www.ipm.ucdavis.edu/PMG/selectnewpest.home.html.

The **Montana State Weed Science Site** maintains a website dealing with noxious weeds of that area of the country. Go to: www.weeds.montana.edu.

The Weed Science Society of America maintains a database with over 200 common American herbs, plants, and weeds, and includes noxious weeds and herbicide resistance. Go to: www.wssa.net.

The mission of **The Entomology and Forest Resources Digital Information Work Group** is to gather, create, maintain, promote the use of, and economically distribute digital information both as resources and as tools to enhance and complement information exchange and educational activities primarily in the fields of entomology, forestry, forest health, and natural resources. Go to: www. bugwood.org.

The Natural Resources Conservation Service is a federal agency that works in partnership with the American people to conserve and sustain our natural resources. Go to: www.nrcs.usda.gov.

The **University of Florida** has provided aquatic weed information since 1979 and appeared on the web back in 1995. Their Aquatic, Wetland, and Invasive Plant Information Retrieval System (APIRS), is the world's largest information resource devoted to that subject. Go to: www.aquat1.ifas.ufl.edu/welcome.html.

In addition, the following books were consulted:

Allan, Mea. *Weeds: The Unbidden Guests in Our Gardens.* New York: The Viking Press, 1978.

Gleason, Henry A. *The New Britton and Brown Illustrated Flora of the Northeastern United States and Adjacent Canada.* New York: The New York Botanical Garden, 1963.

Hitchcock. A. S. *Manual of the Grasses of the United States.* New York: Dover Publications, Inc., 1971.

Niering, William A., and Olmstead, Nancy C. *The Audubon Society Field Guide to North American Wildflowers, Eastern Region.* New York: Alfred A. Knopf, 1979.

Spellenberg, Richard A. *The Audubon Society Field Guide to North American Wildflowers, Western Region.* New York: Alfred A. Knopf, 1979.

Appendix II

Suppliers

The Japan Woodworker, 1731 Clement Avenue, Alameda, CA 94501; (800) 537–7820; www.japanwoodworker.com. If you'd like an Asian touch for the garden, these are some of the most aesthetic weeders ever made.

Lee Valley Tools Ltd., P.O. Box 1780, Ogdensburg, NY 13669; (800) 871-8158; www.leevalley.com. A good selection of cultivators and weeding tools.

Mellinger's Inc., 2310 West South Range Road, North Lima, OH 44452; (800) 321–7444; www.mellingers.com. Not quite soup to nuts, but a good supplier of handheld weeders.

Peaceful Valley Farm, P.O. Box 2209, Grass Valley, CA 95945; (888) 784–1722; www.groworganic.com. A dependable mail-order supplier of a number of gardening tools, including the entire line of flamers for weed control.

Walt Nicke Company, P.O. Box 433, Topsfield, MA 01983; (978) 887–3388; www.gardentalk.com. Probably one of the first mail-order garden supply sites in the country and it still carries a wide line of weeding supplies.

Index

275